Nature & Art Editions

Relaxing Forest Mandalas

Mindfulness Coloring Book

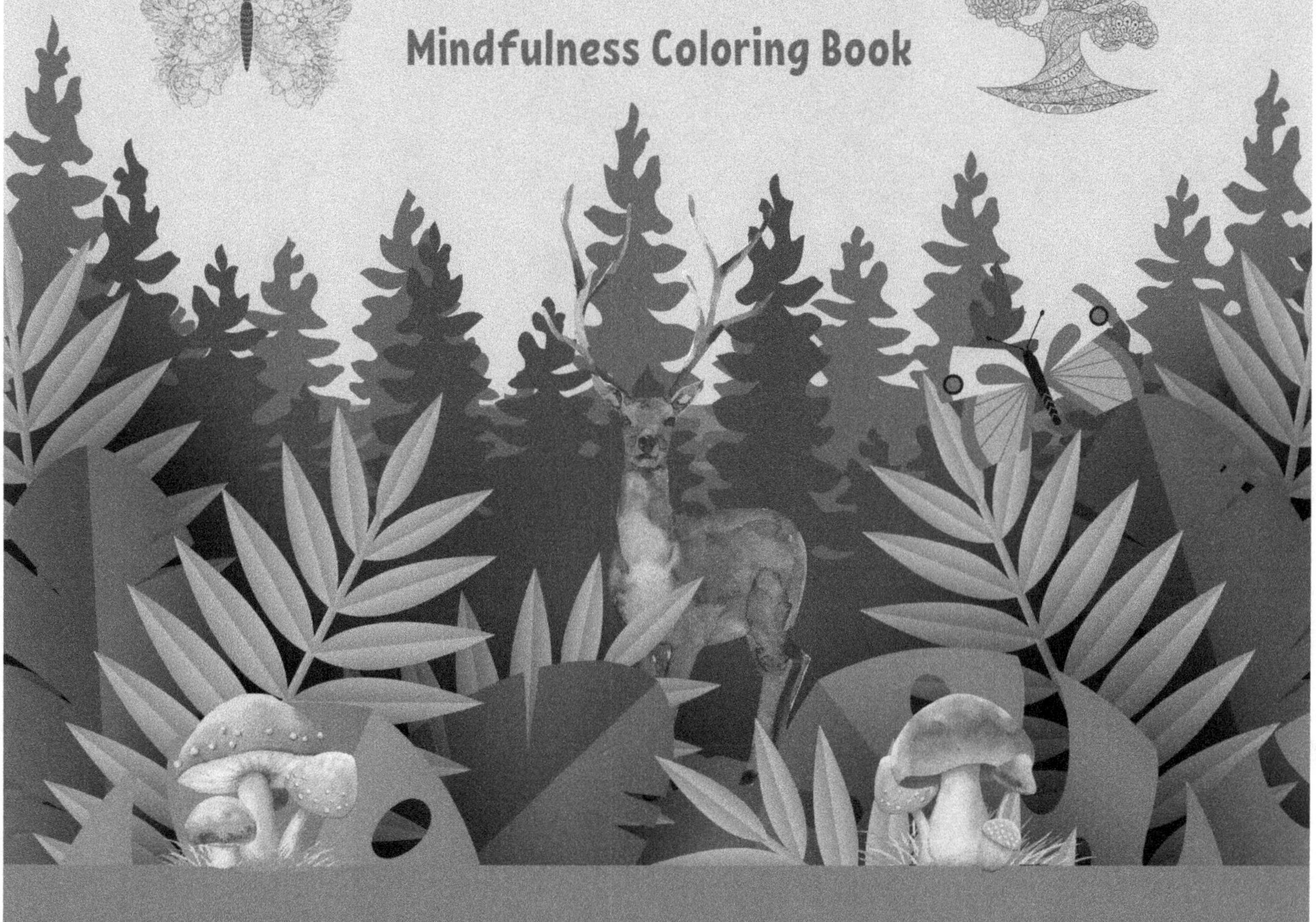

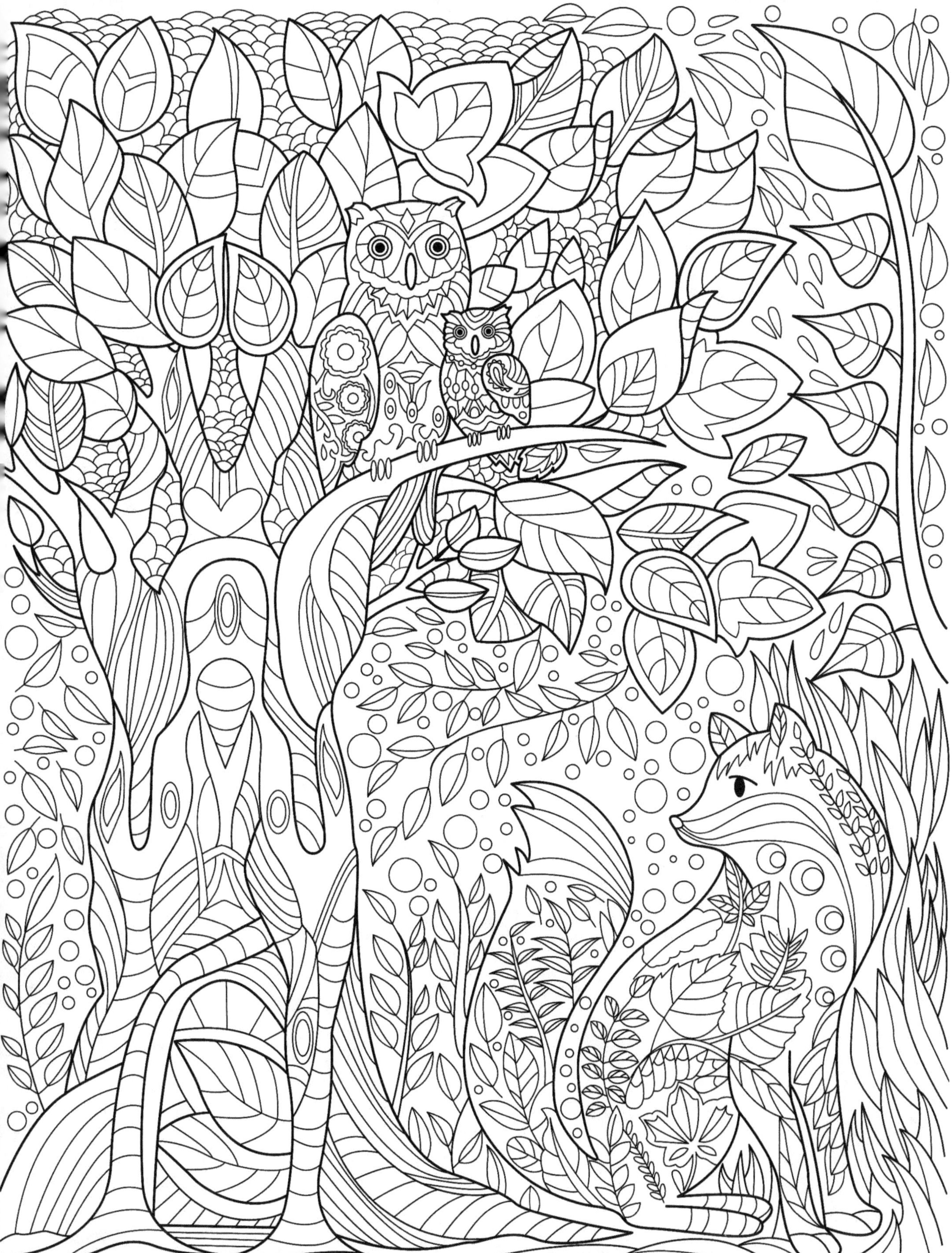

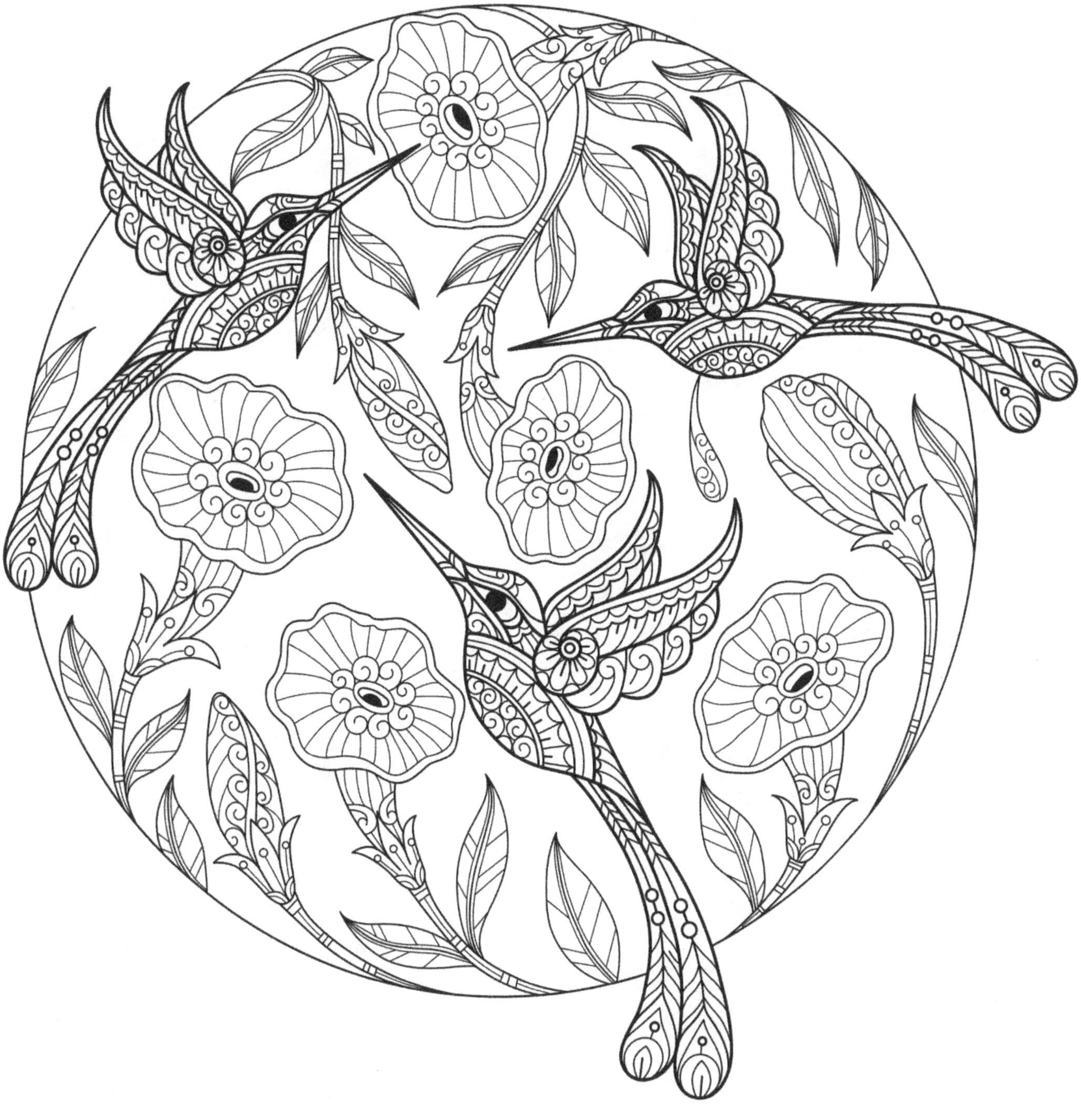

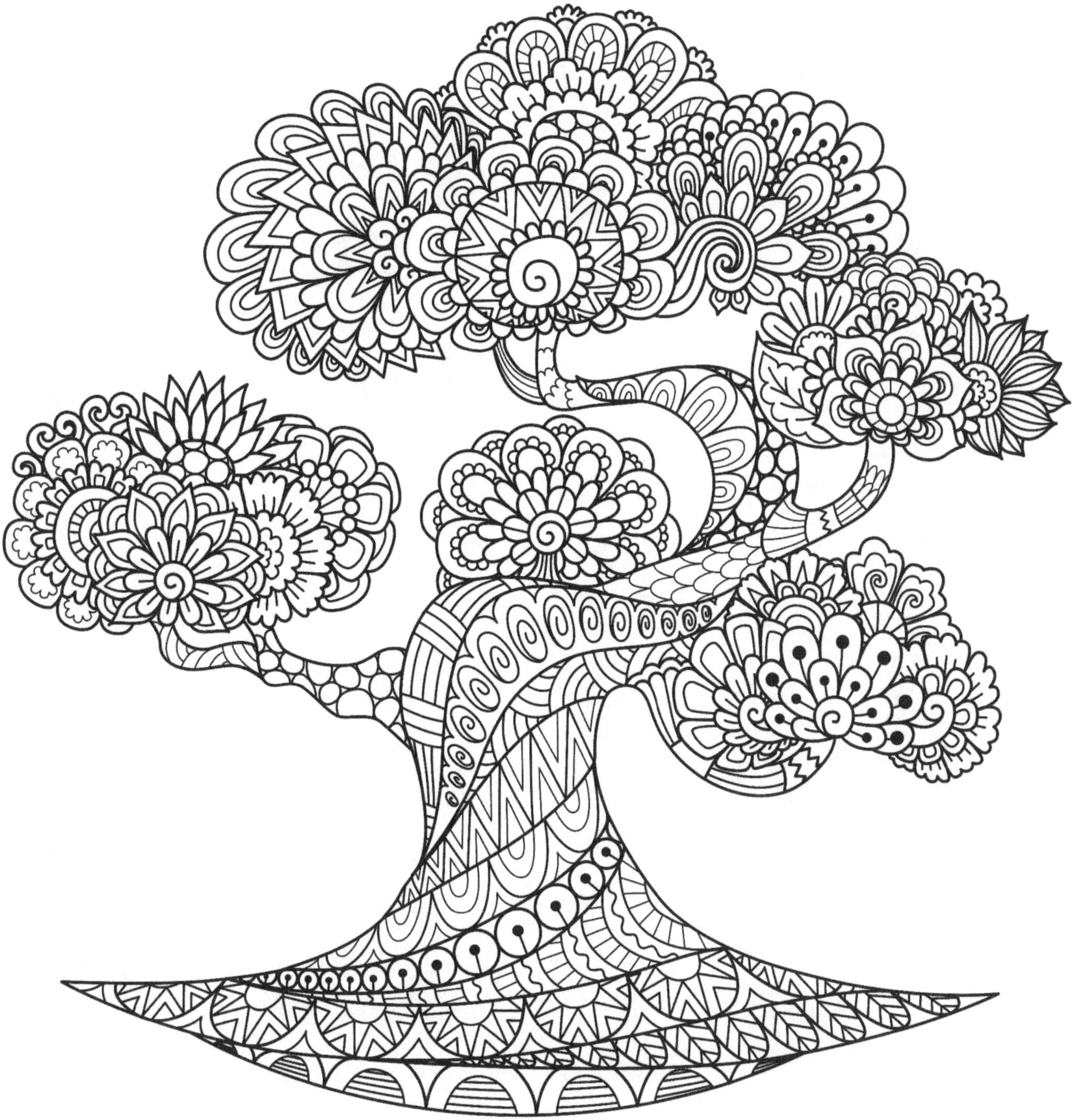

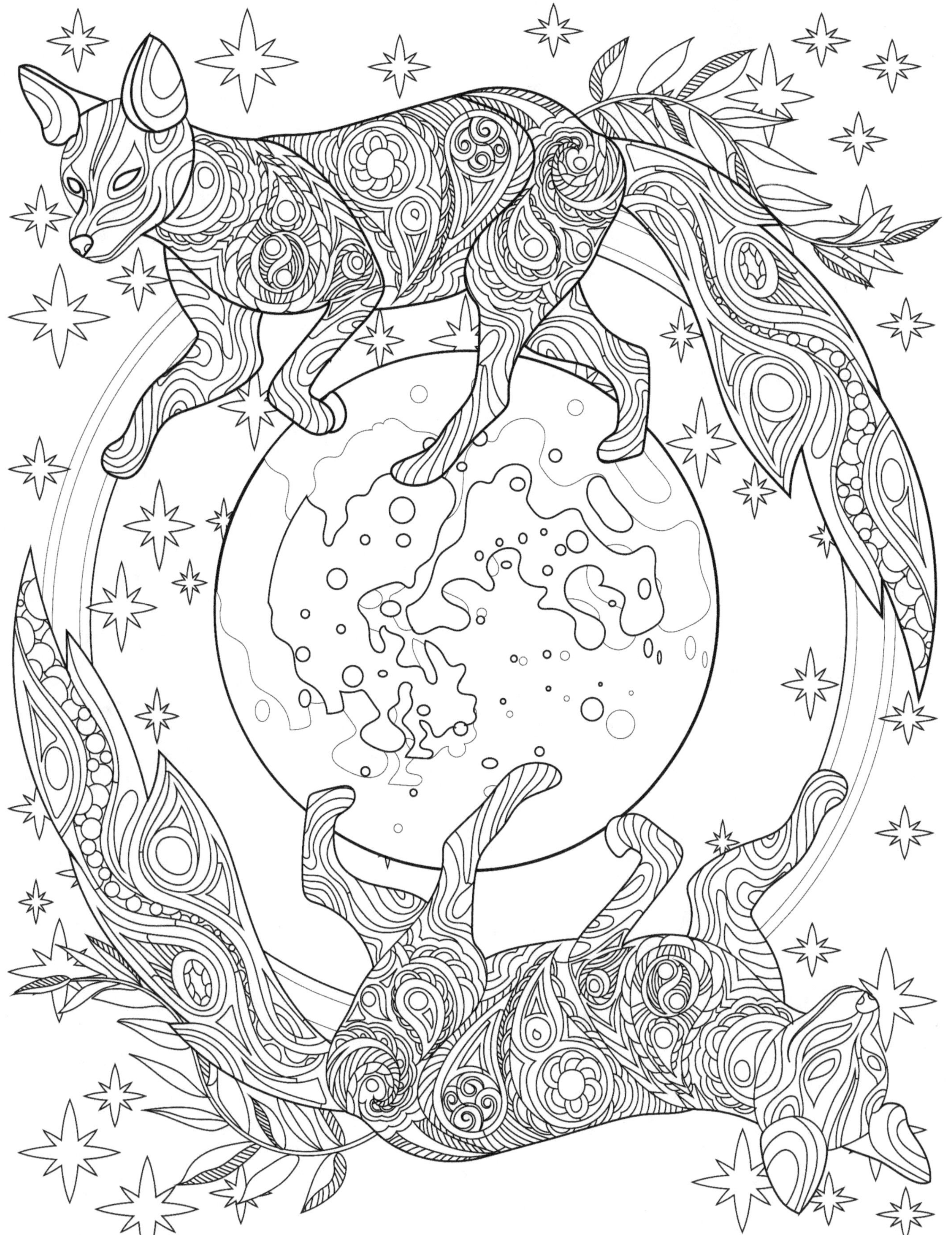

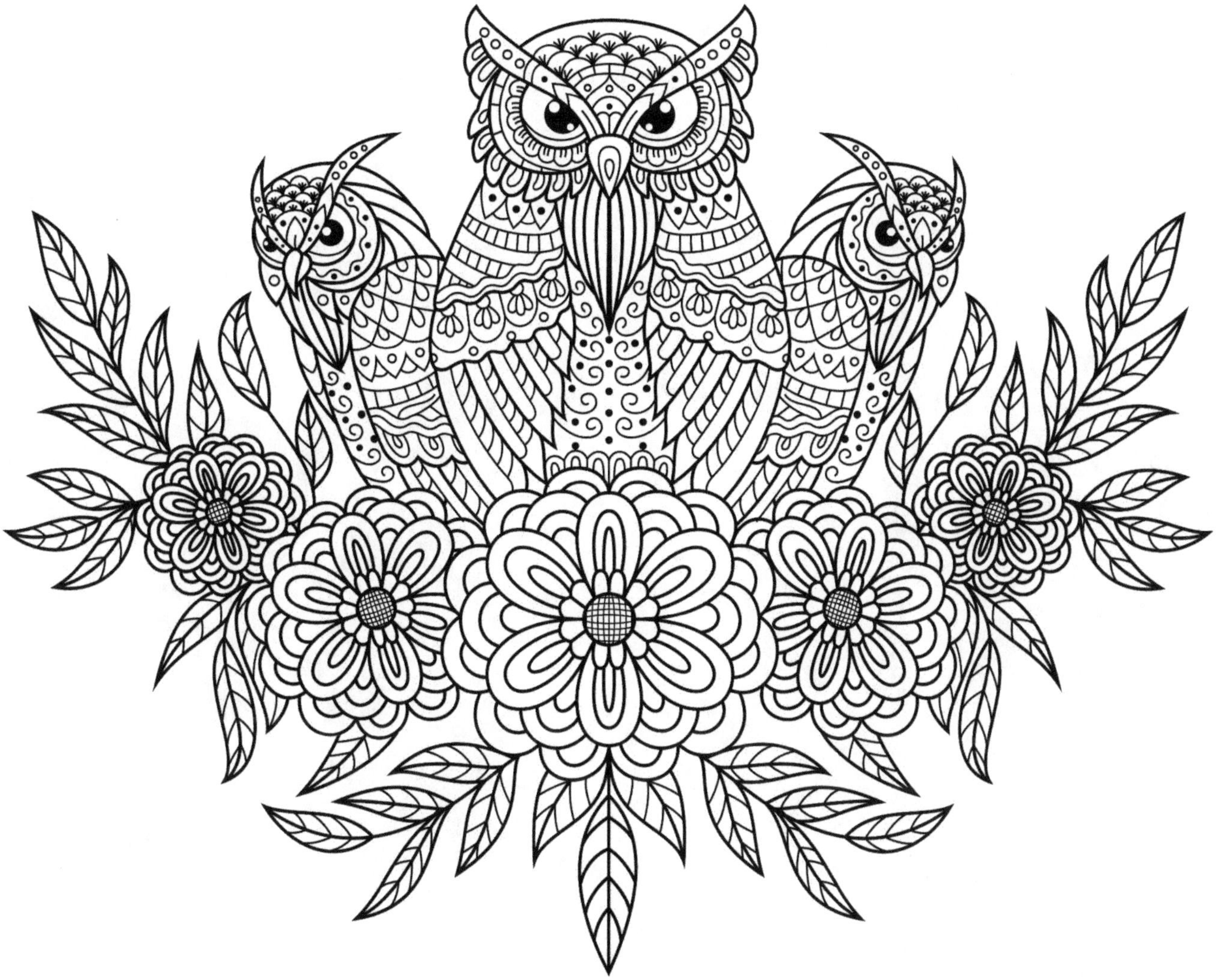

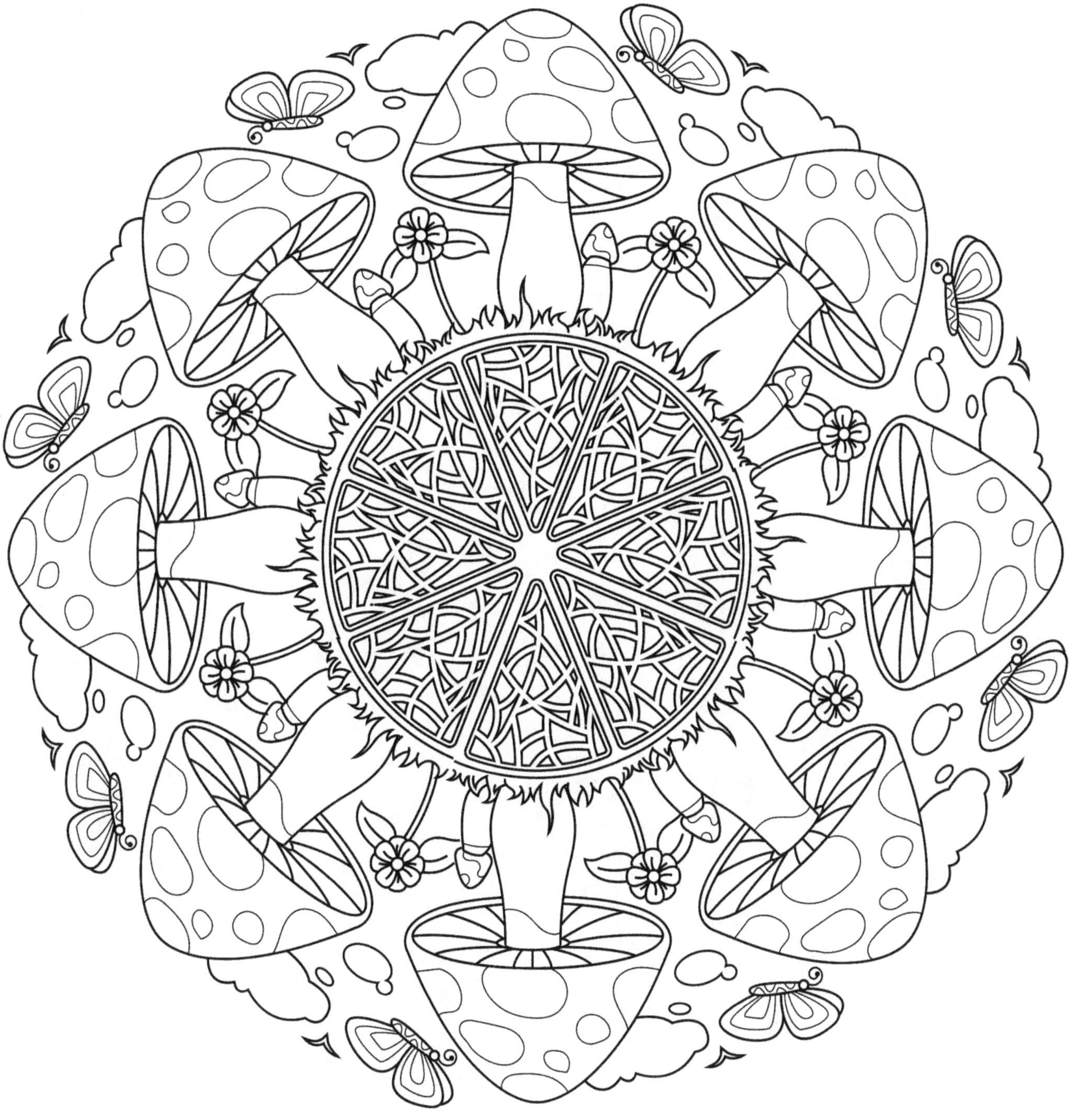

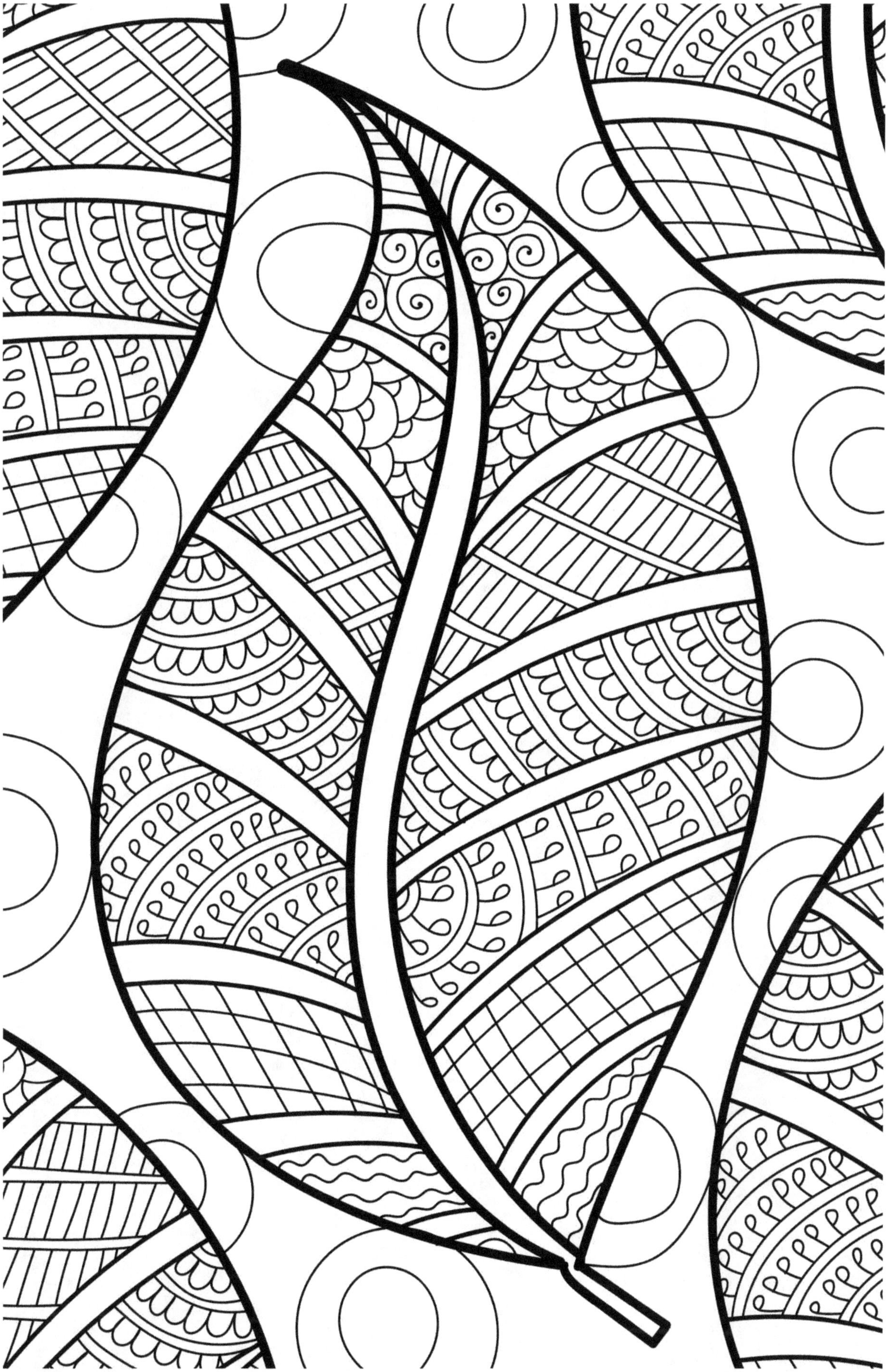

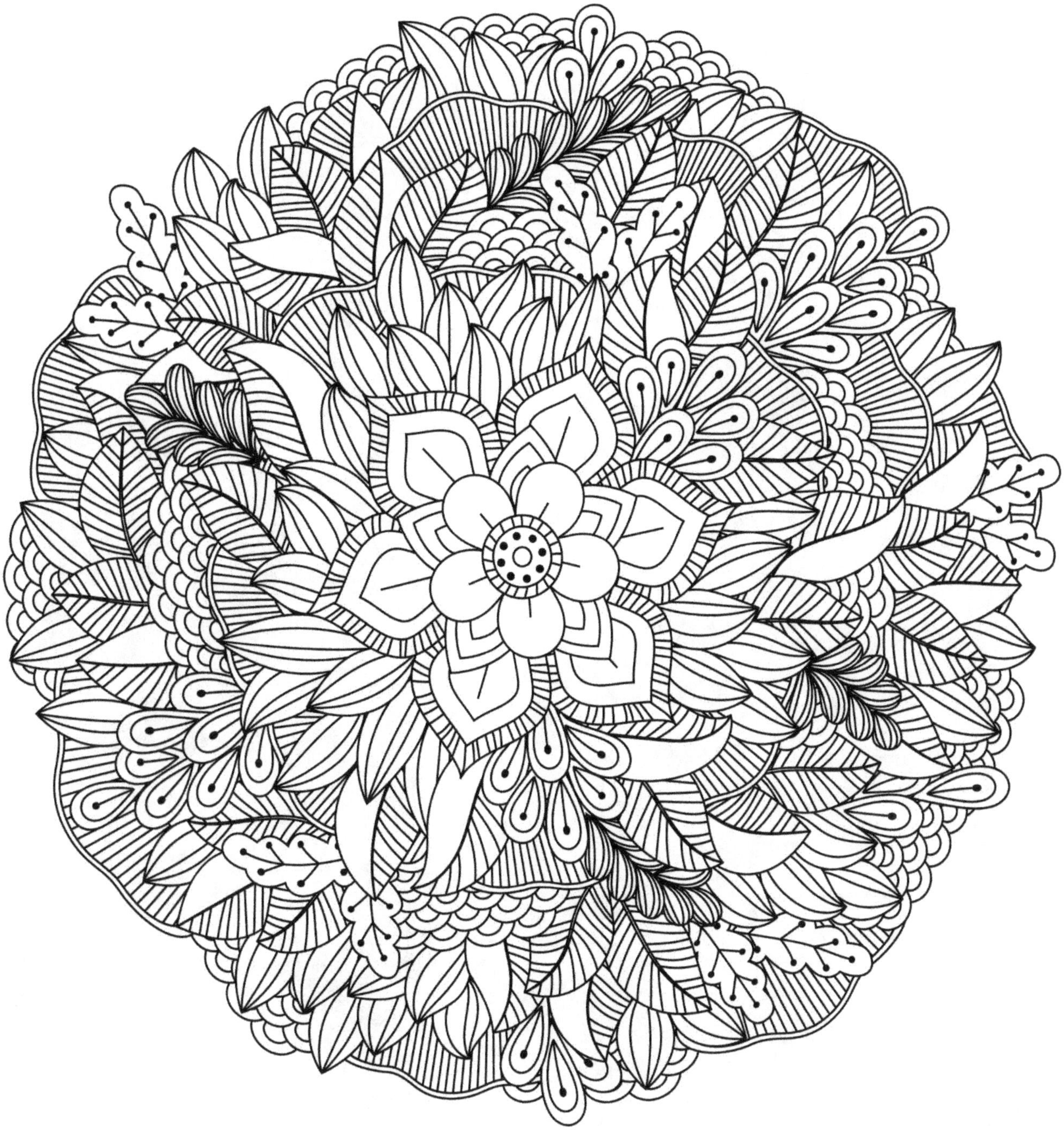

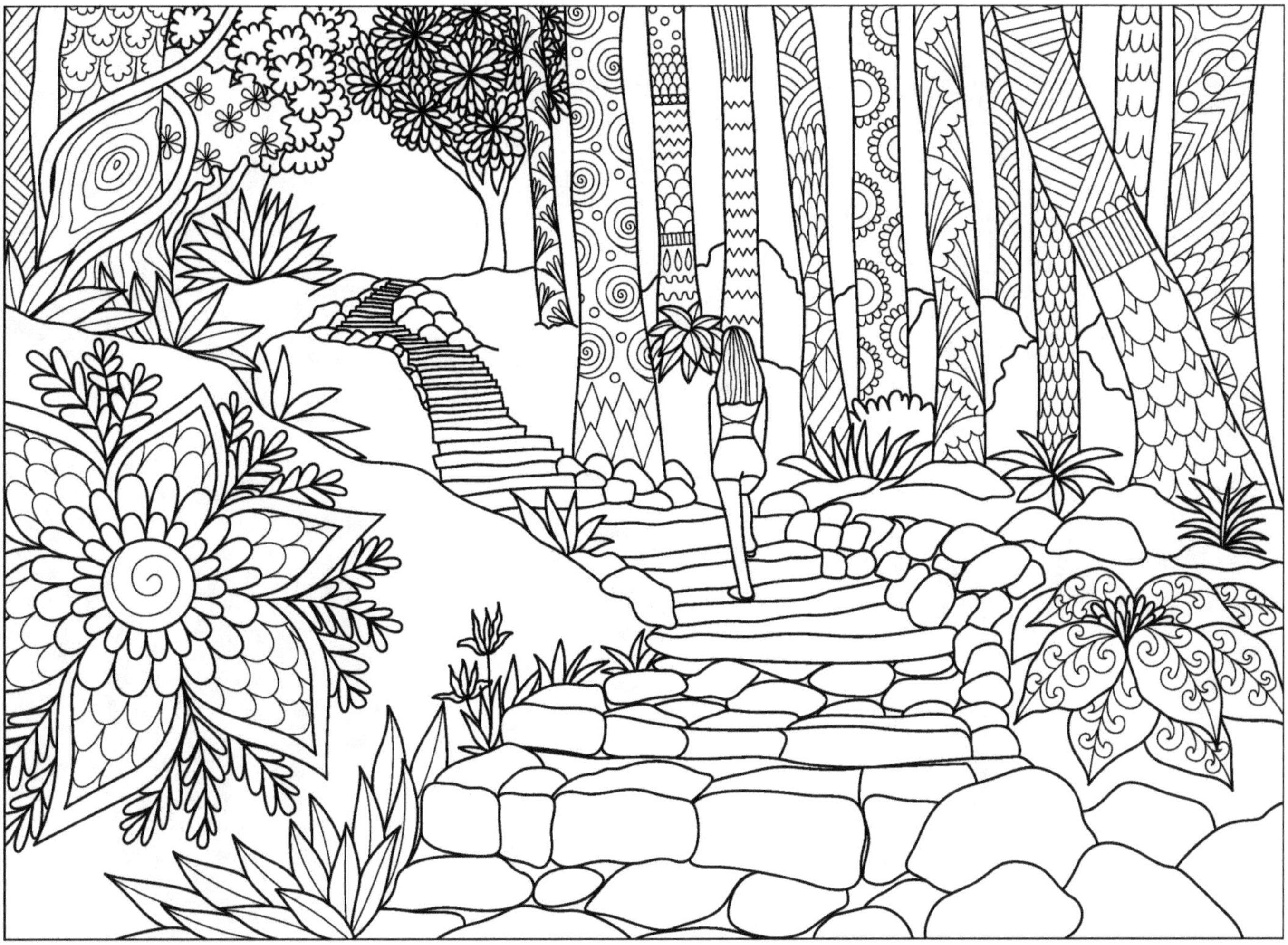

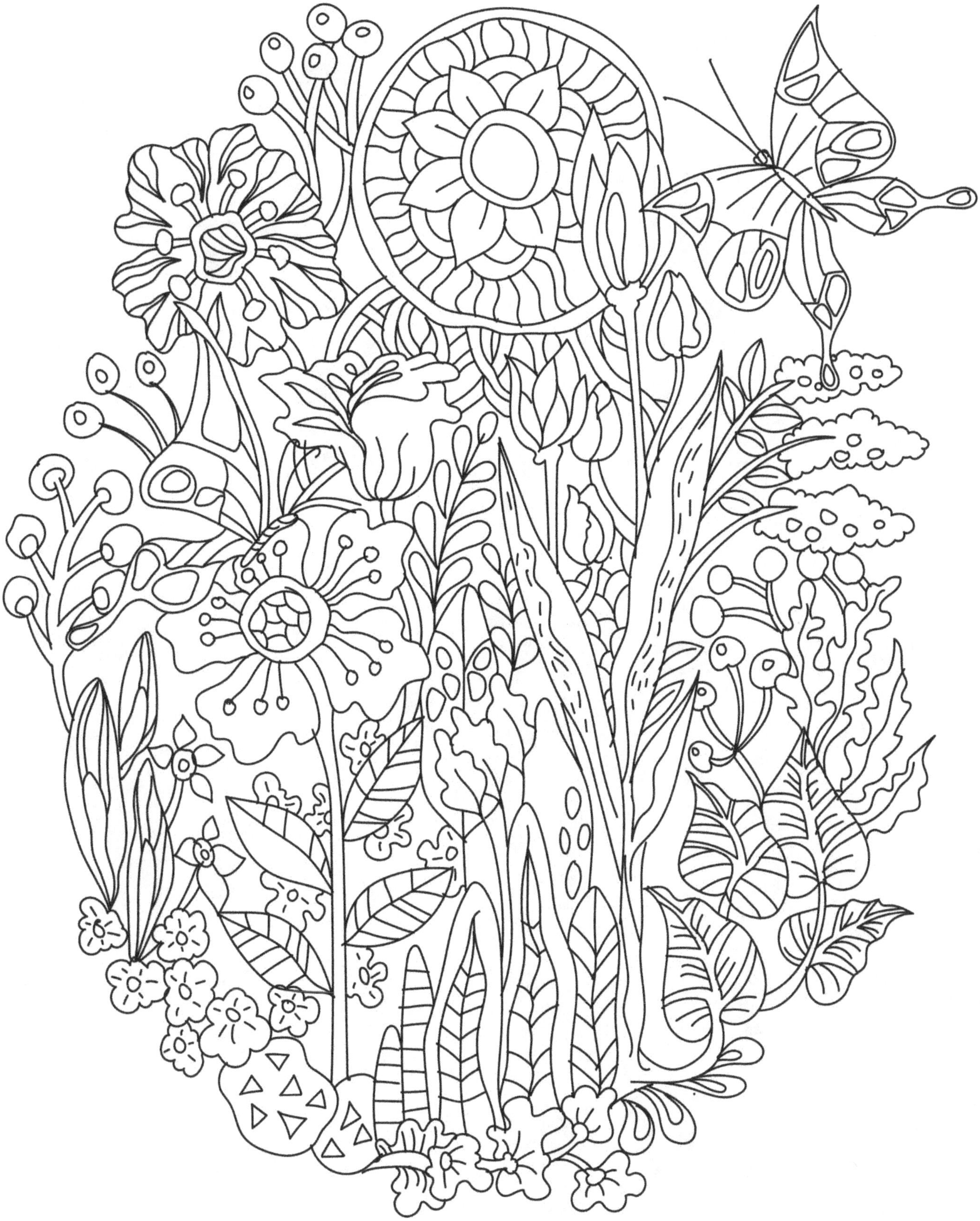

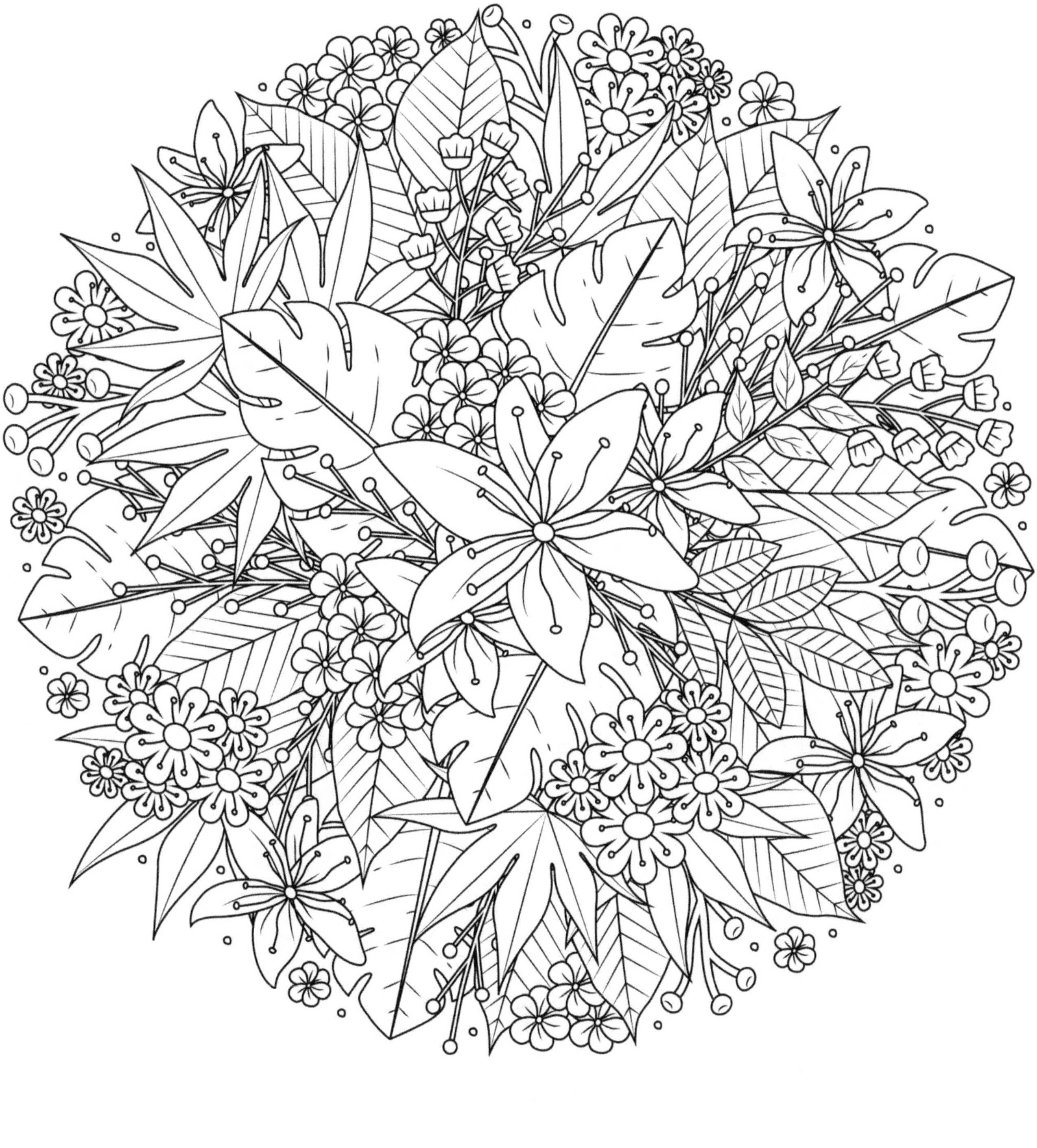

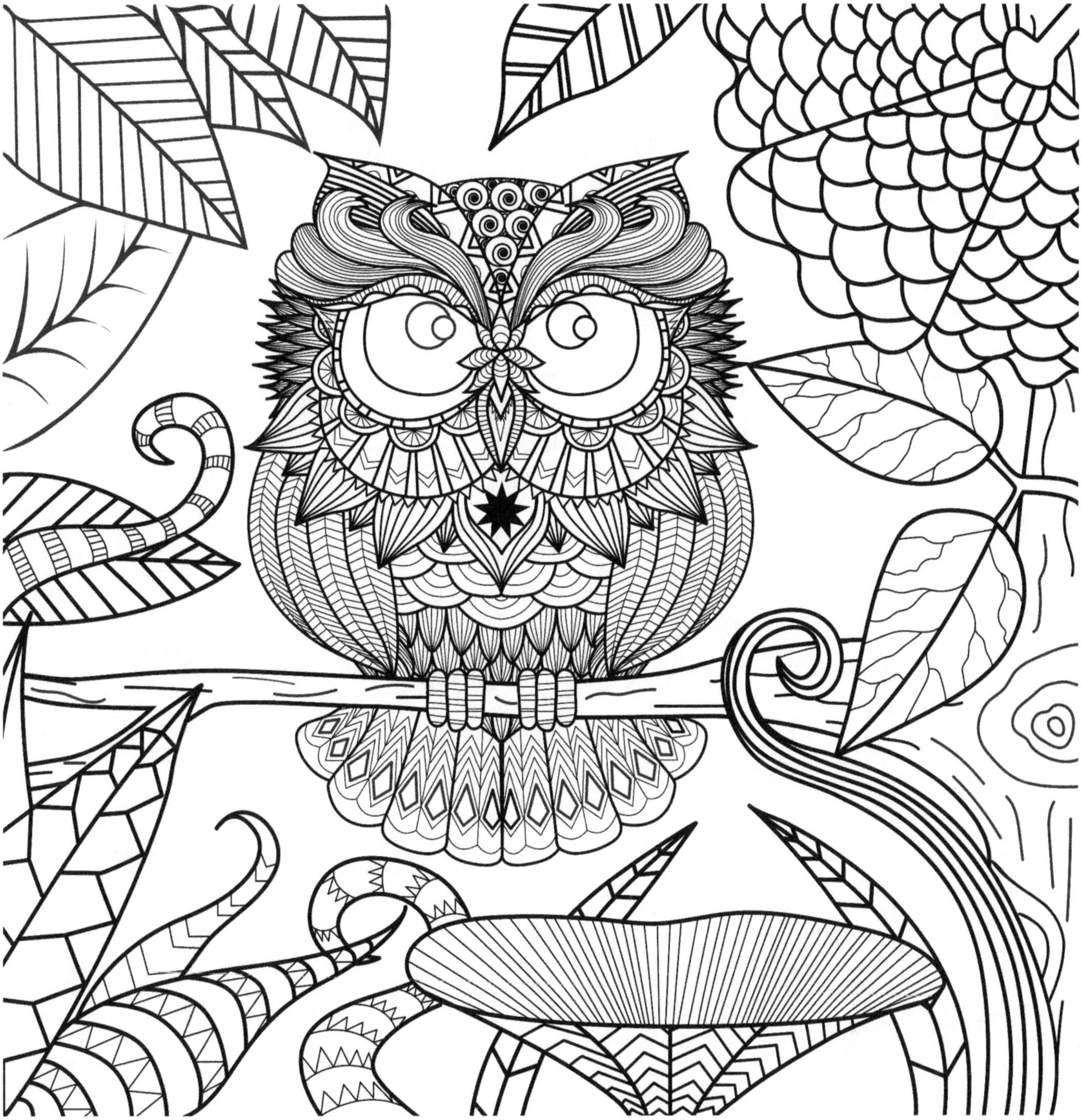

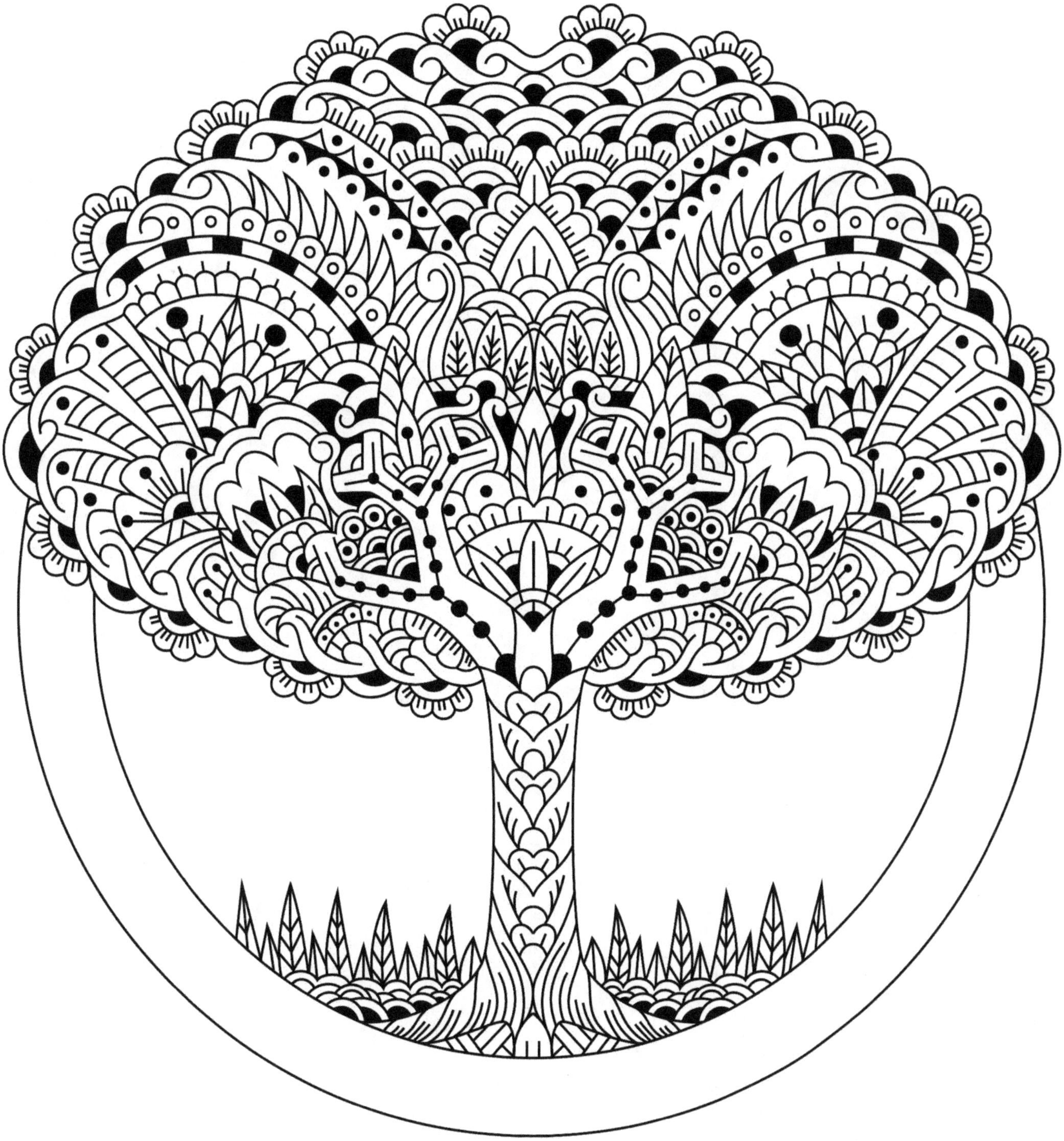

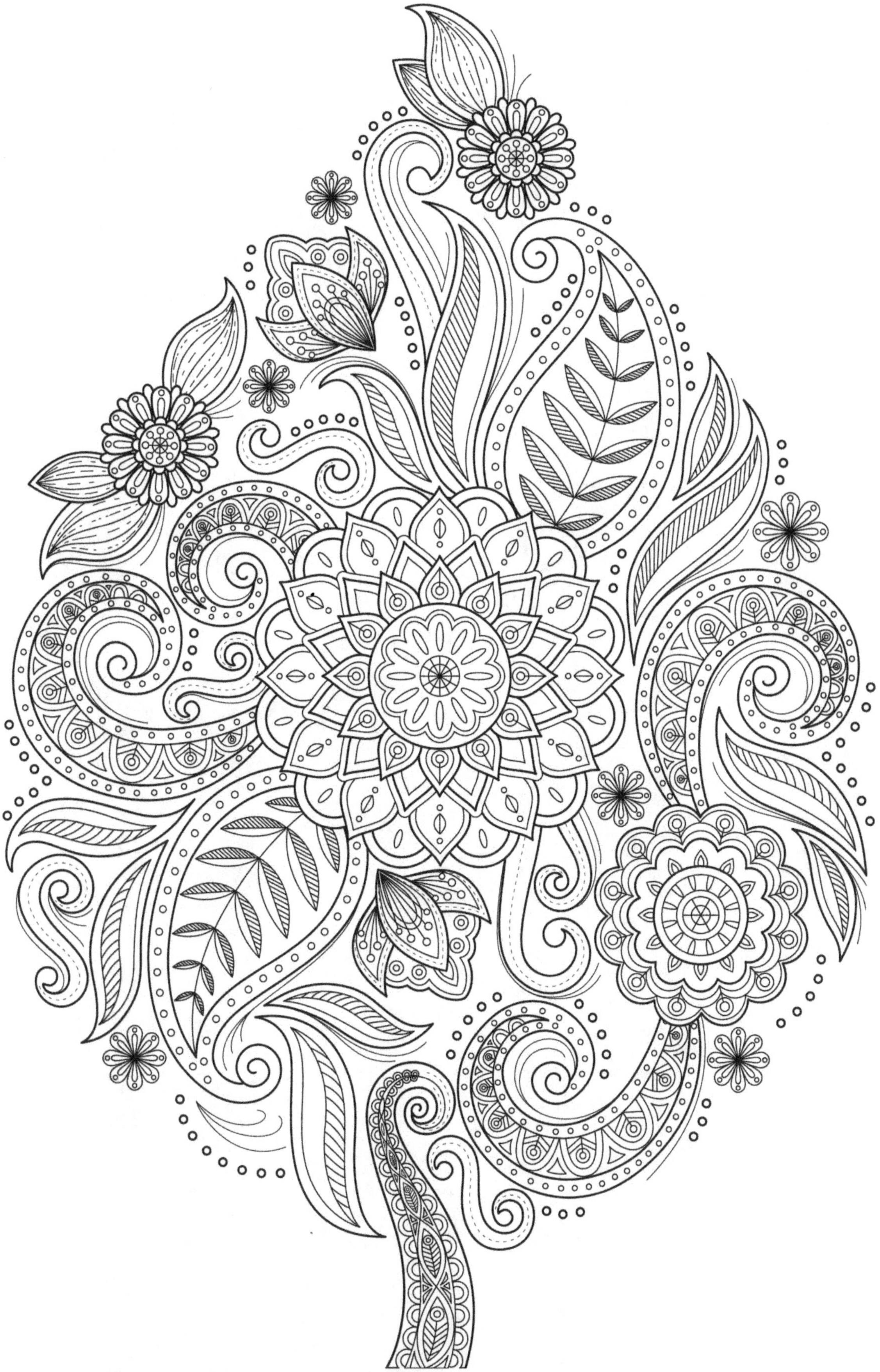

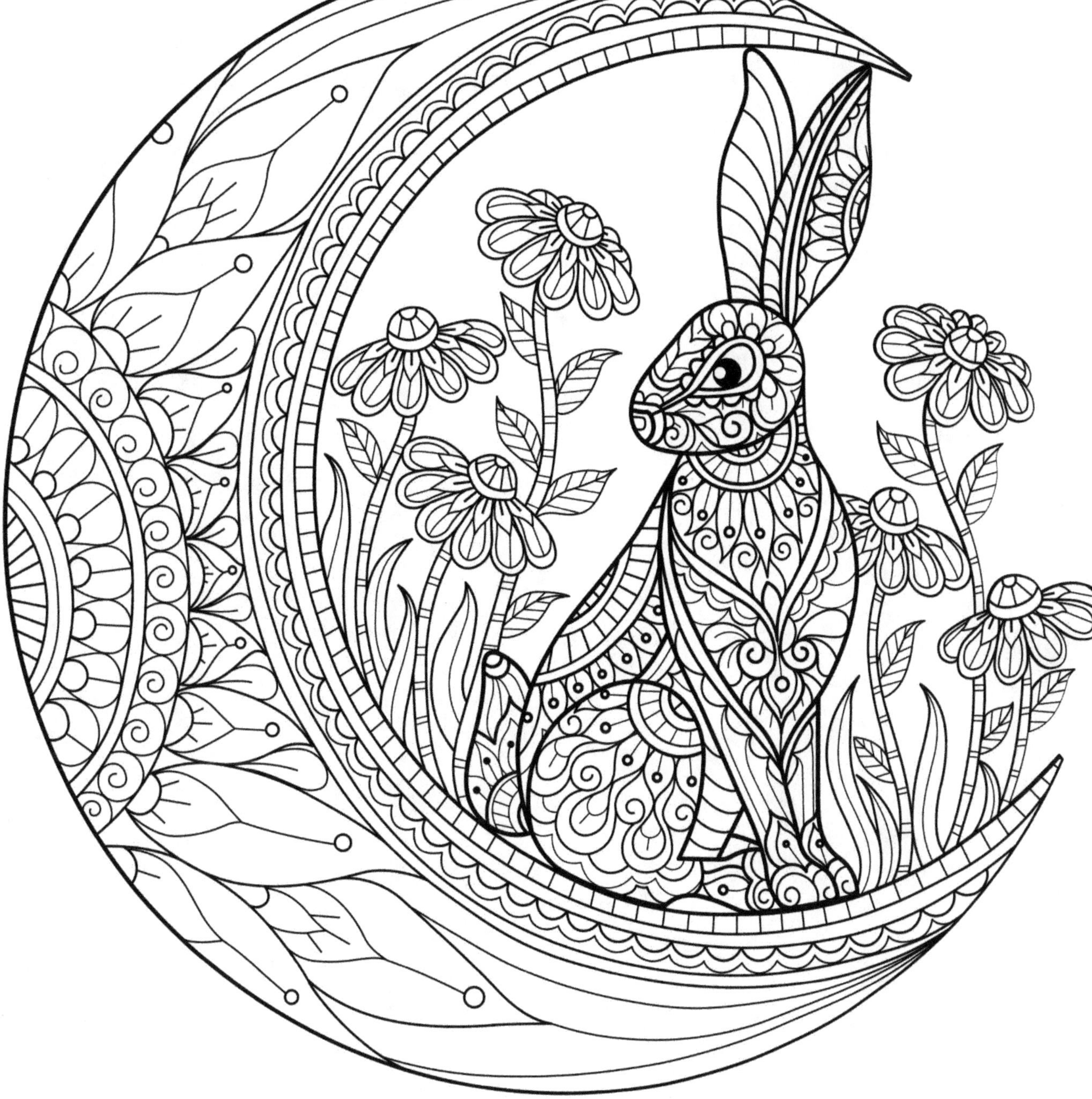

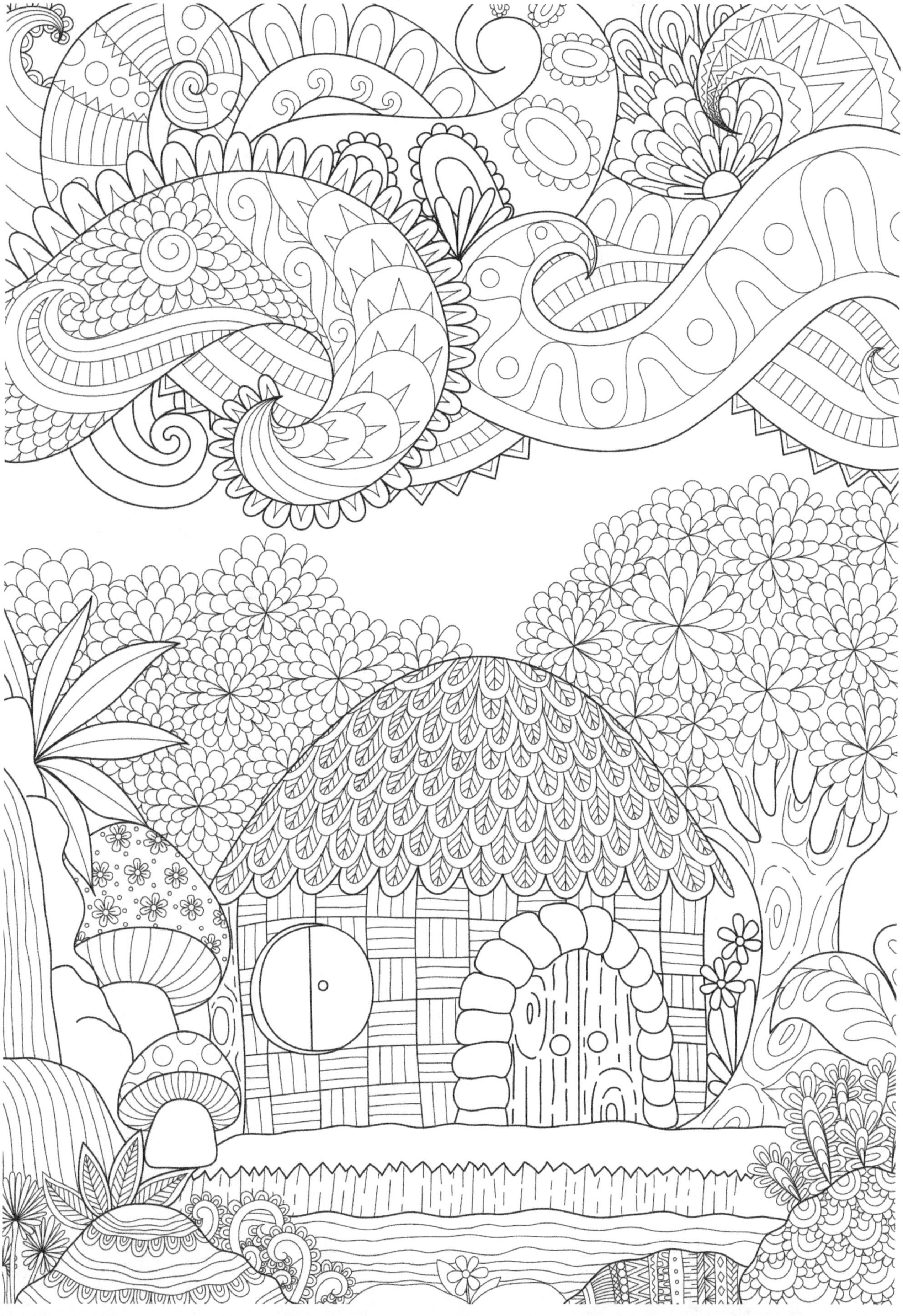

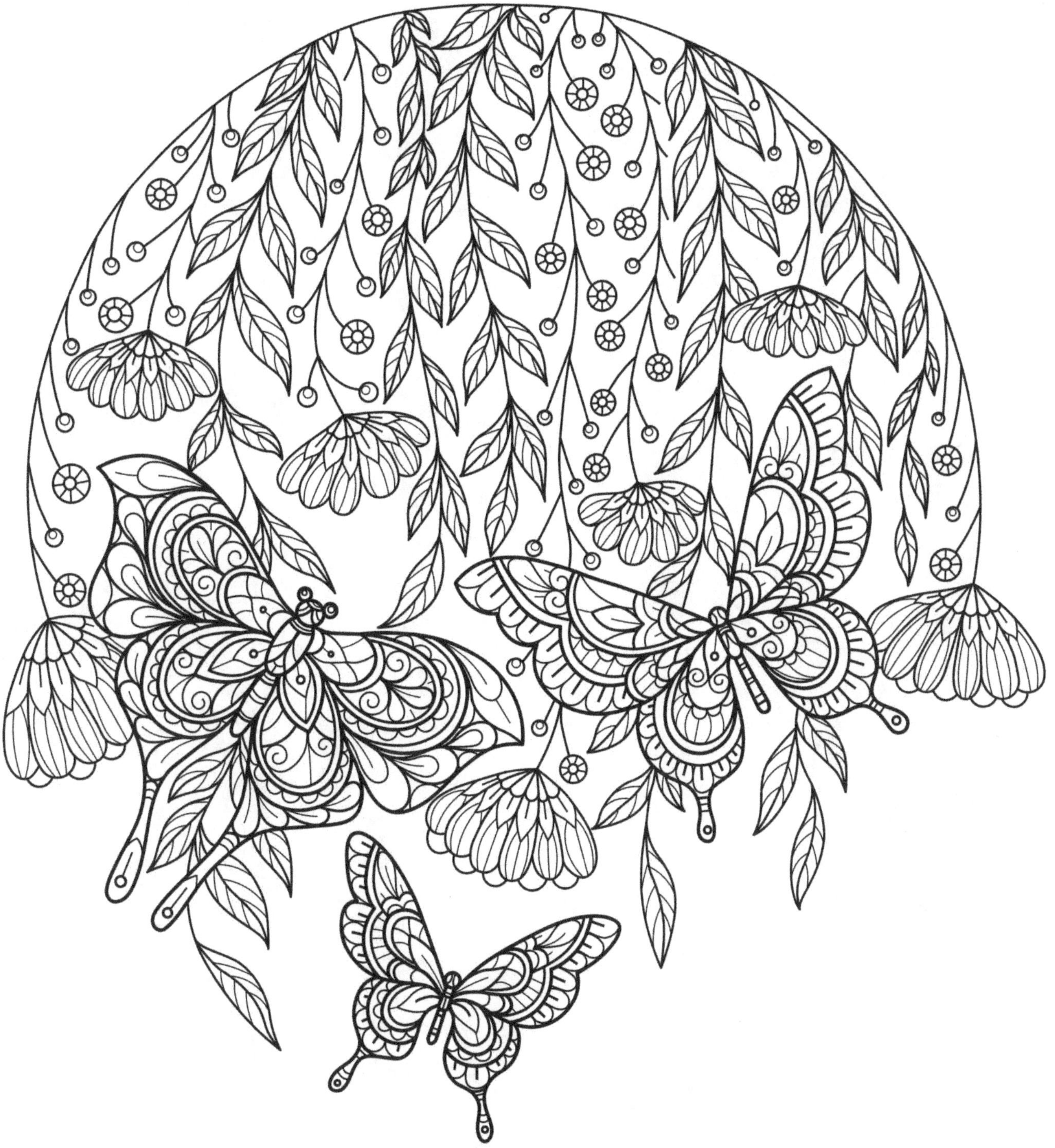

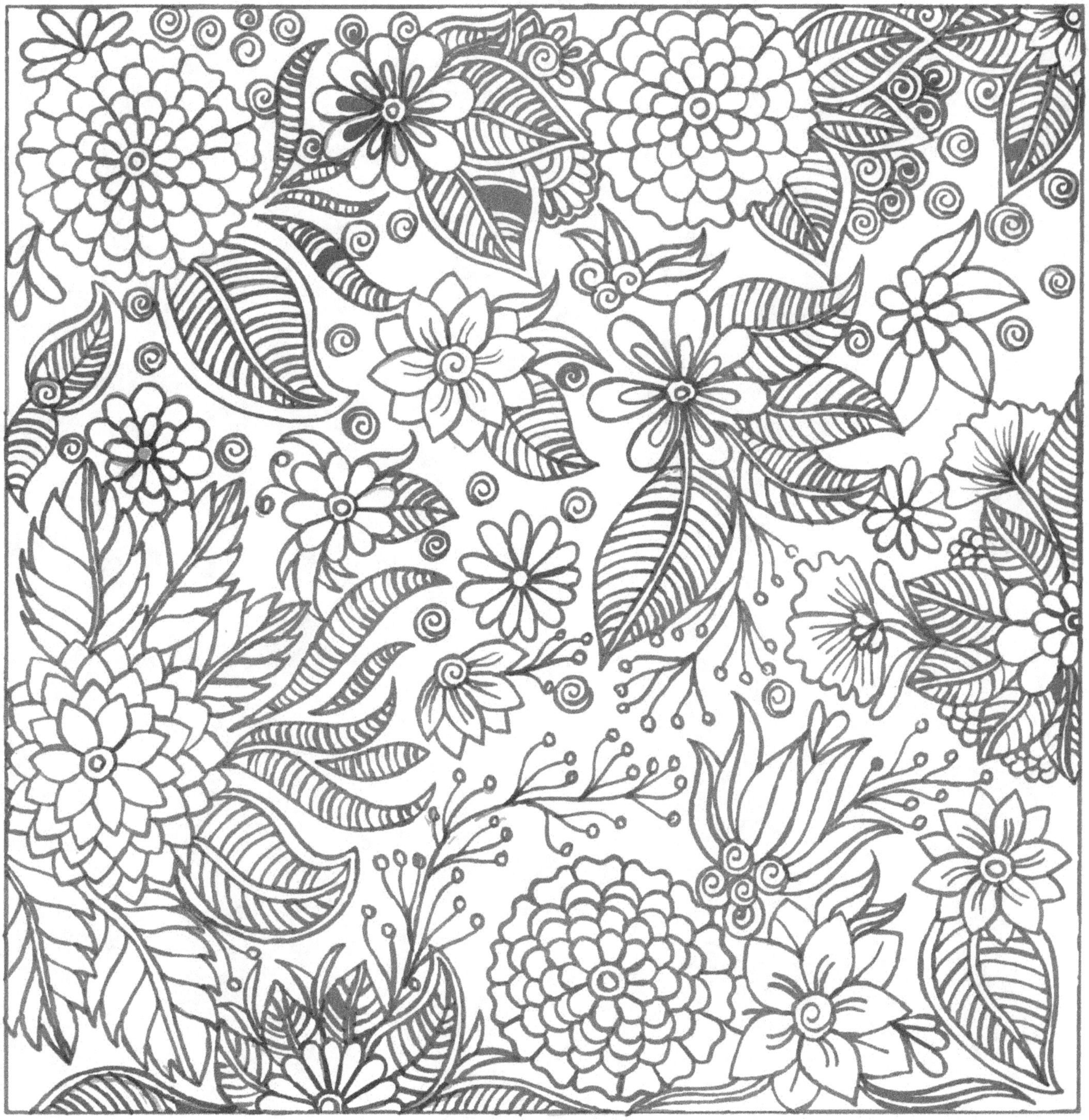

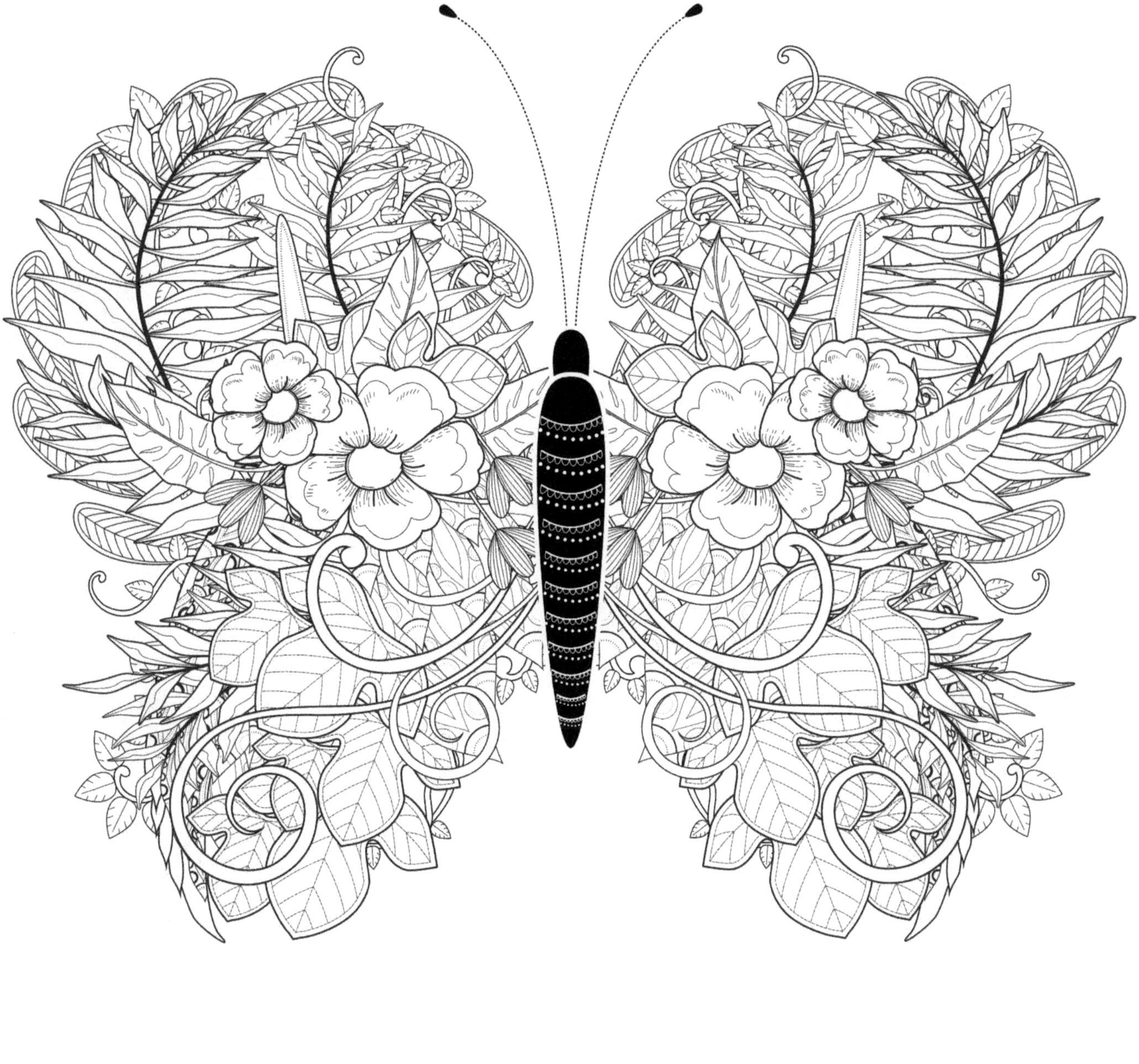

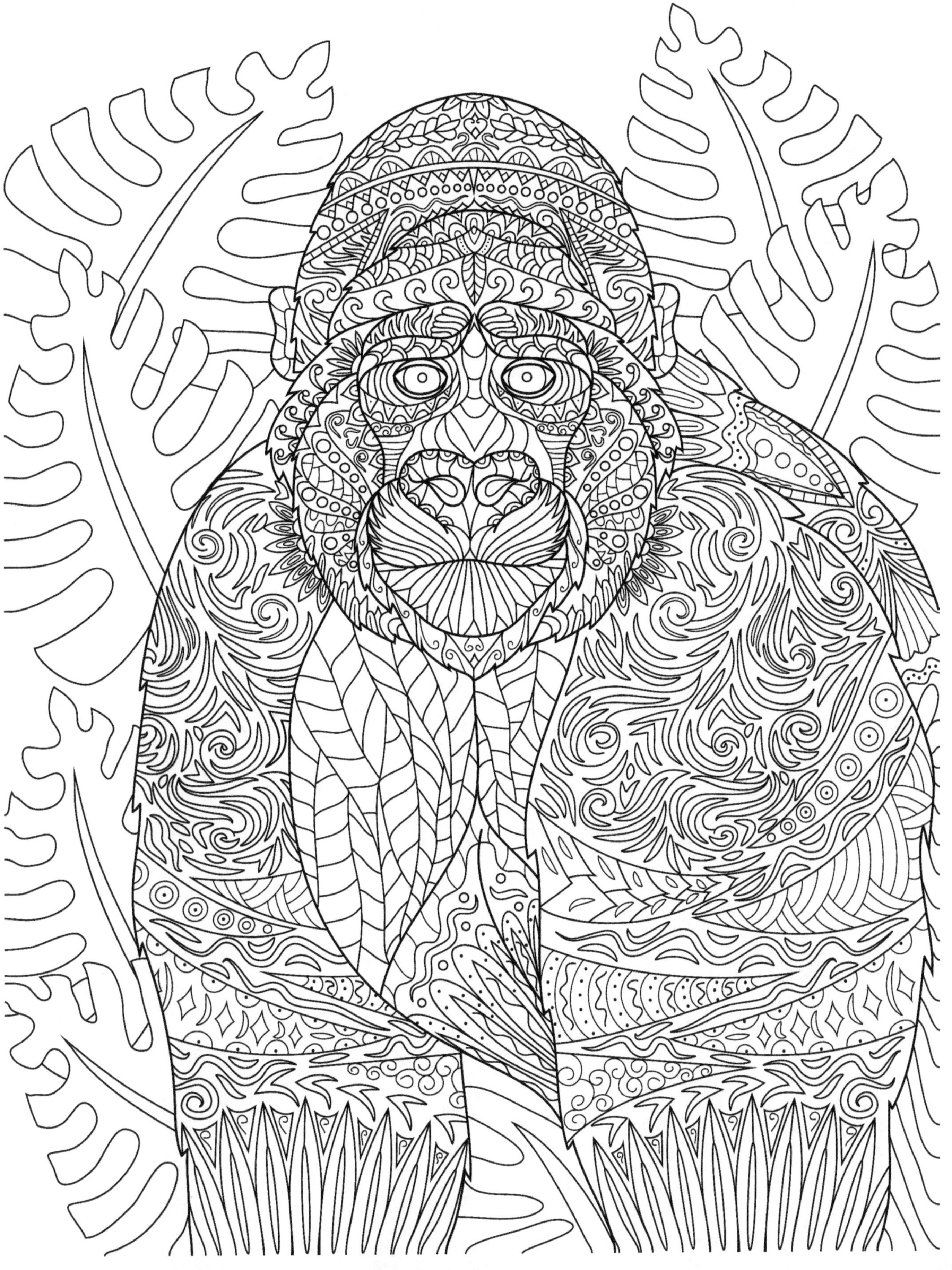

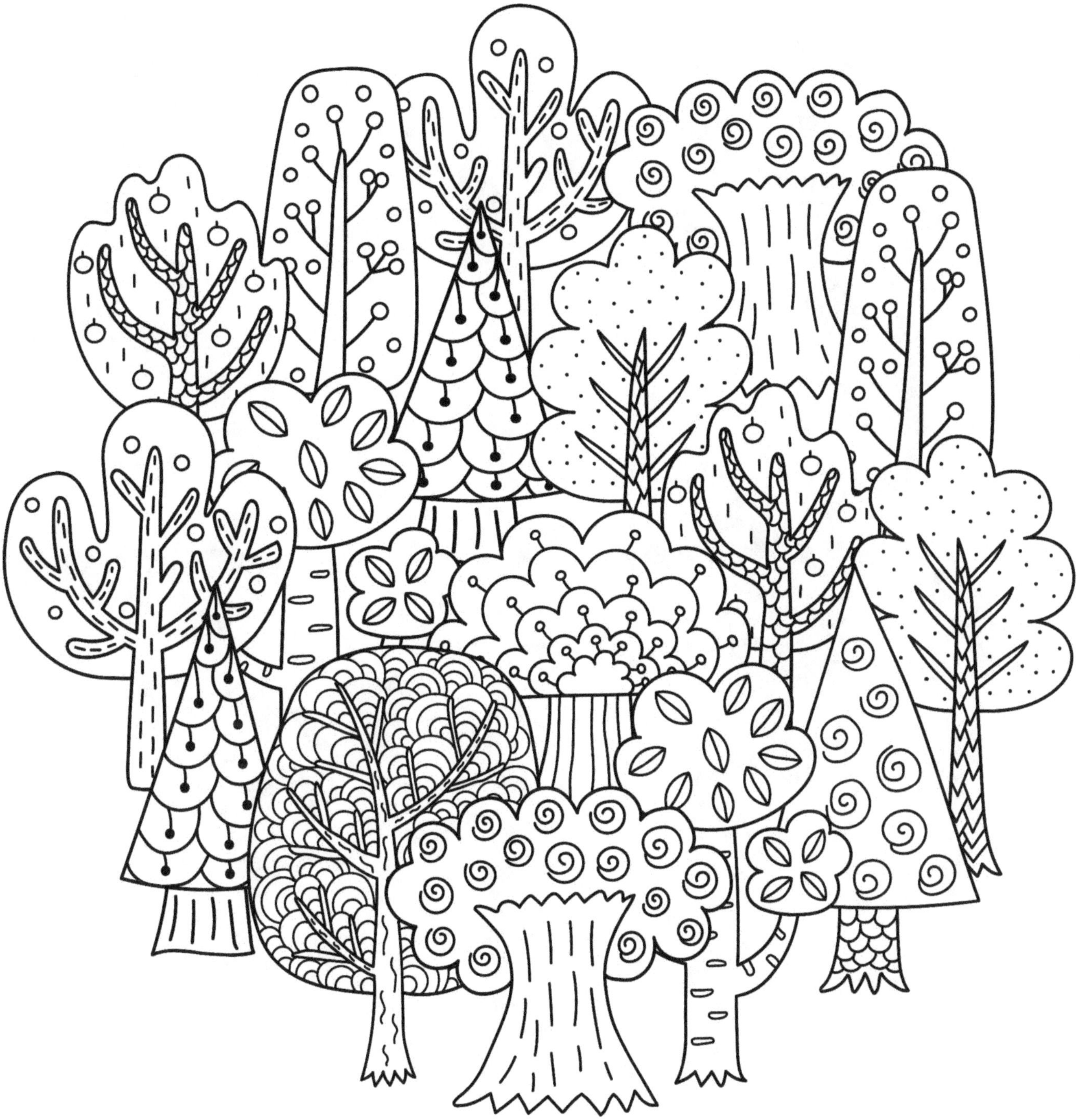

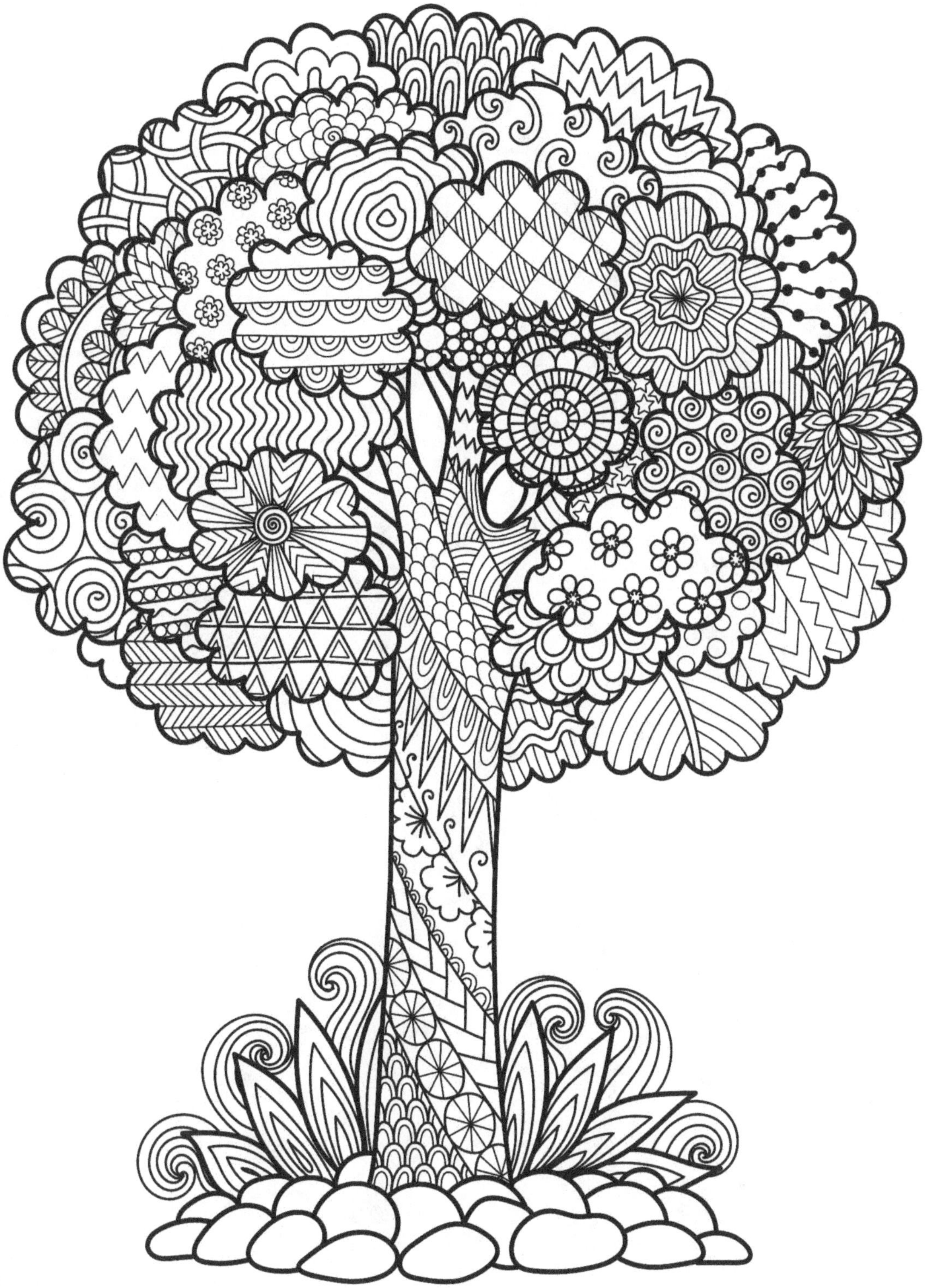

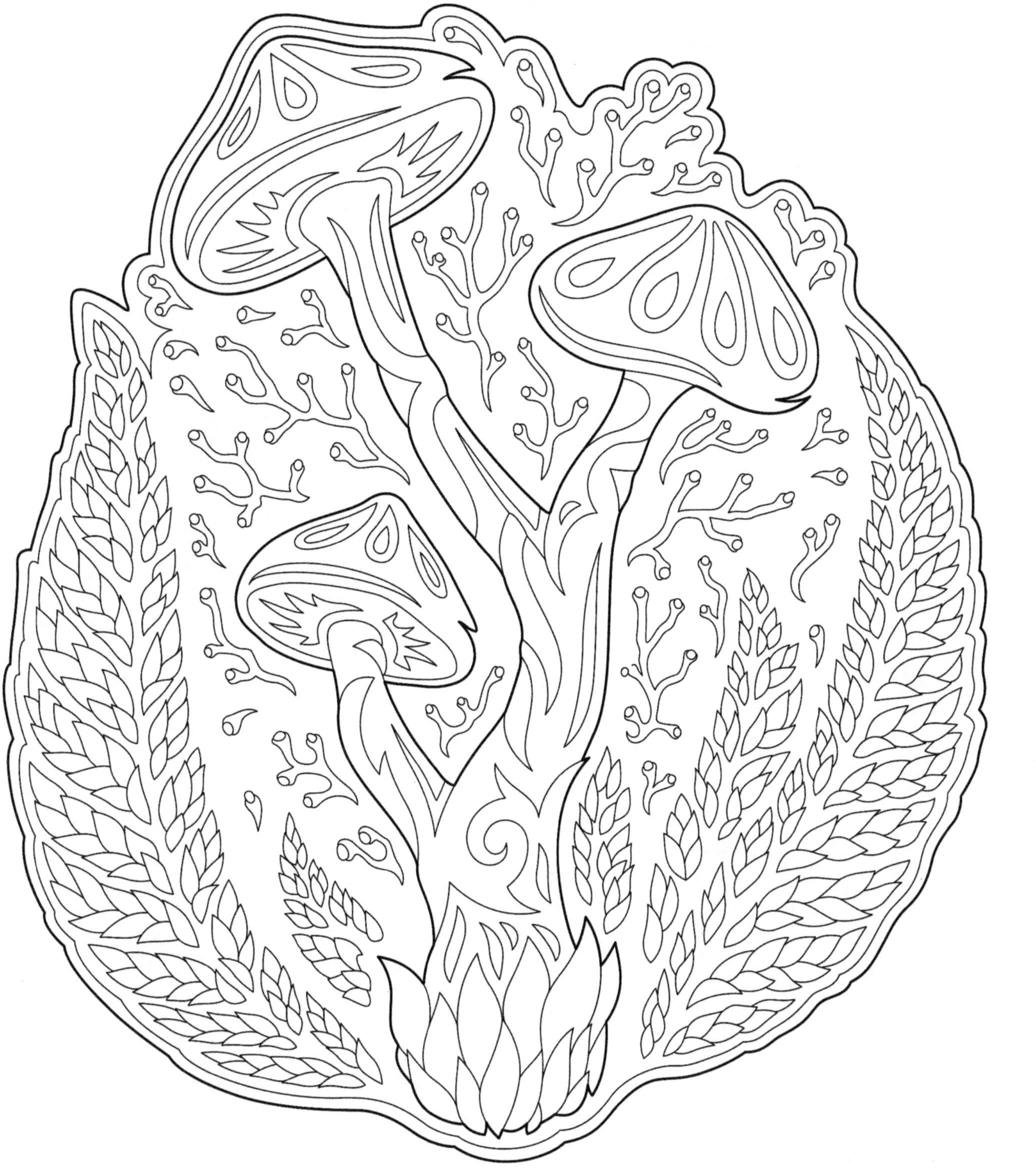

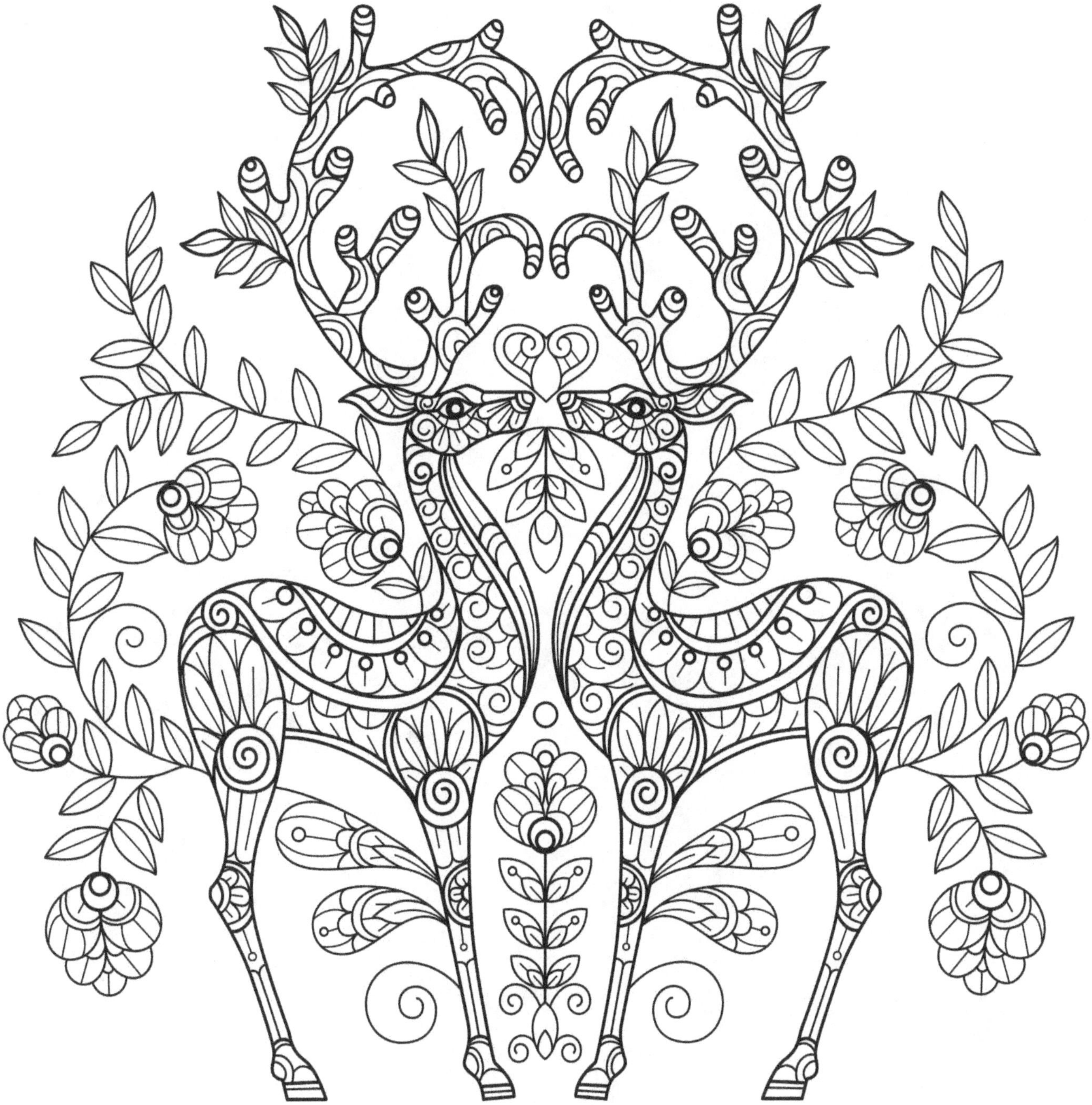

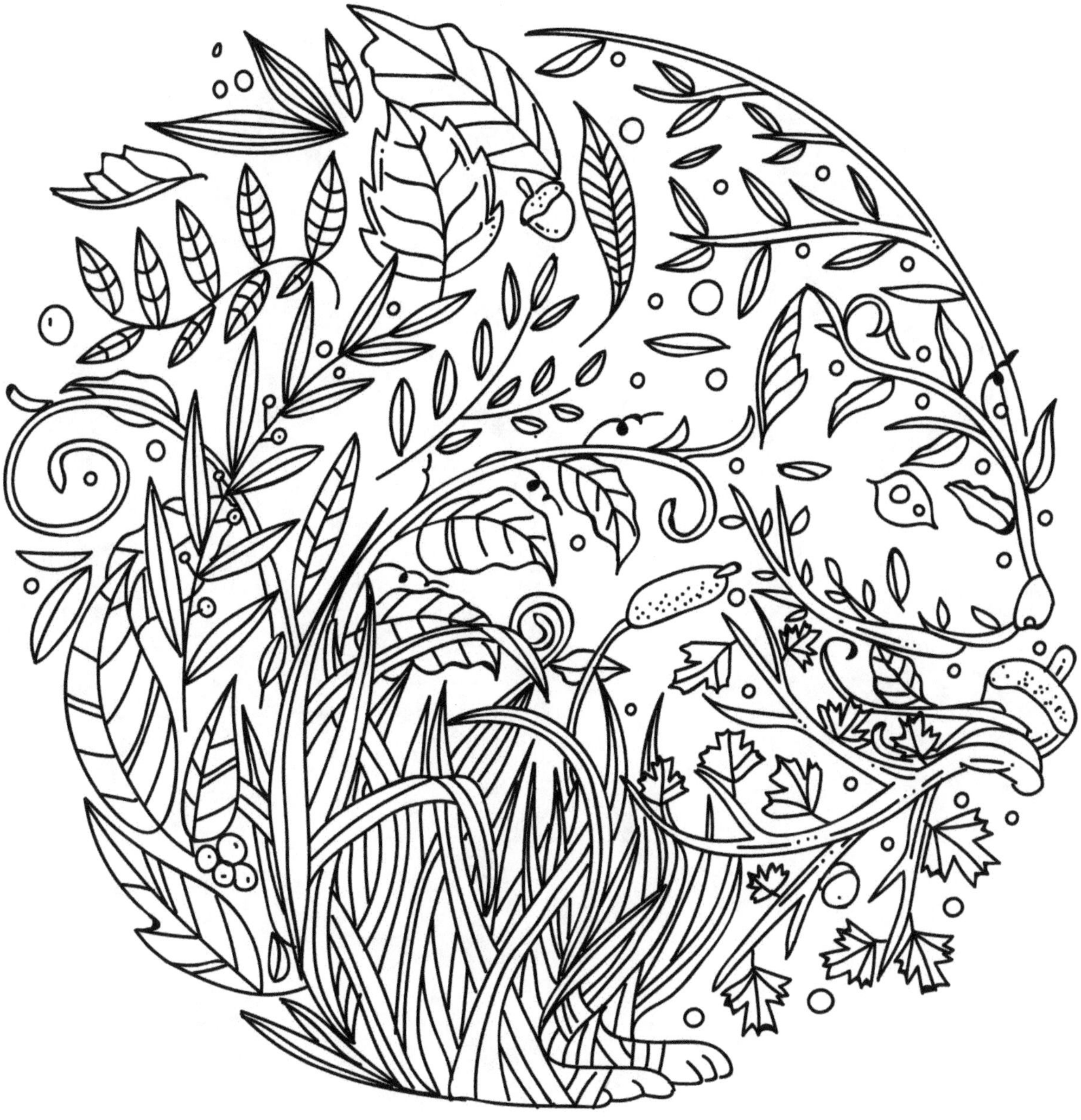

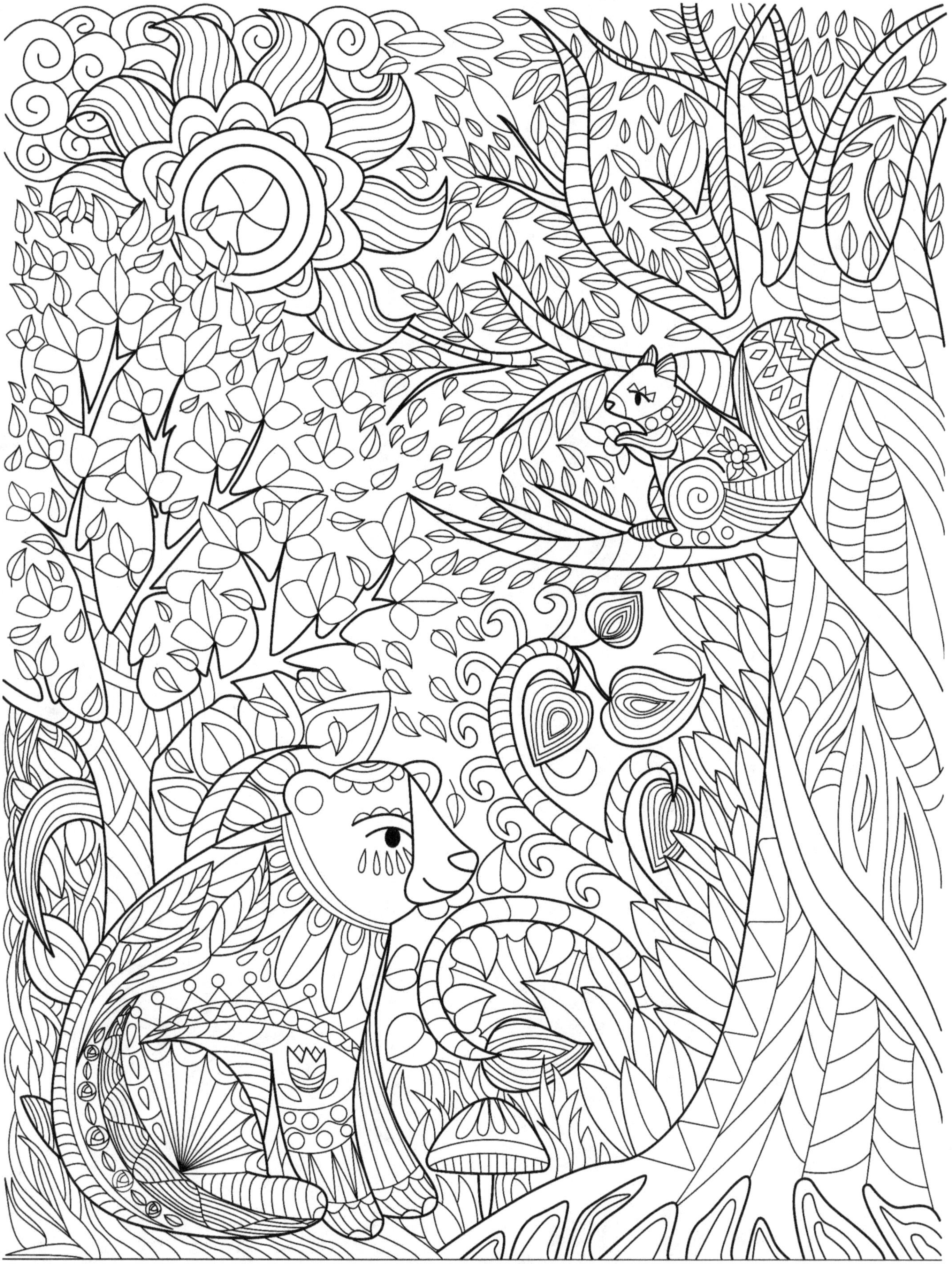

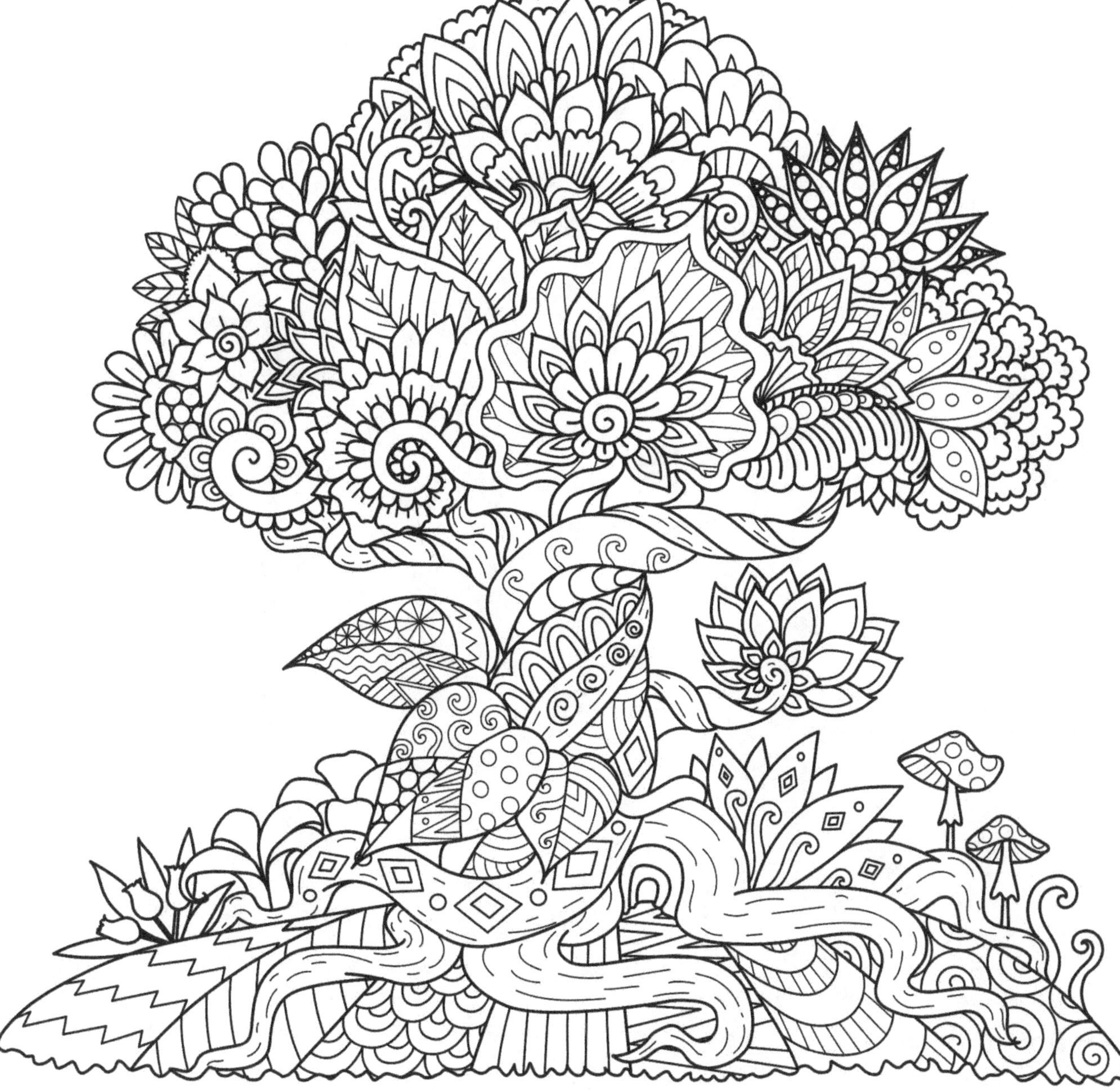

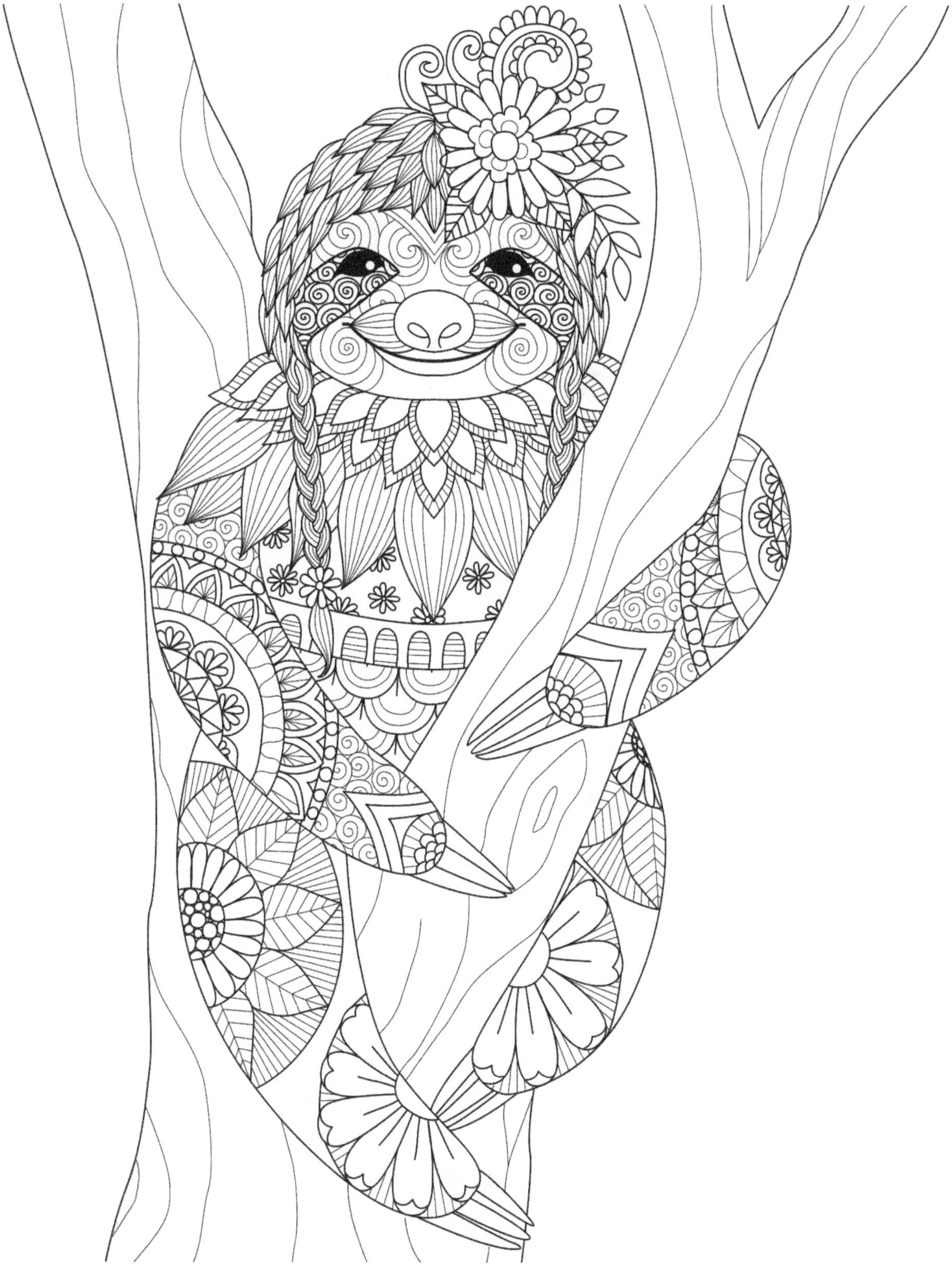

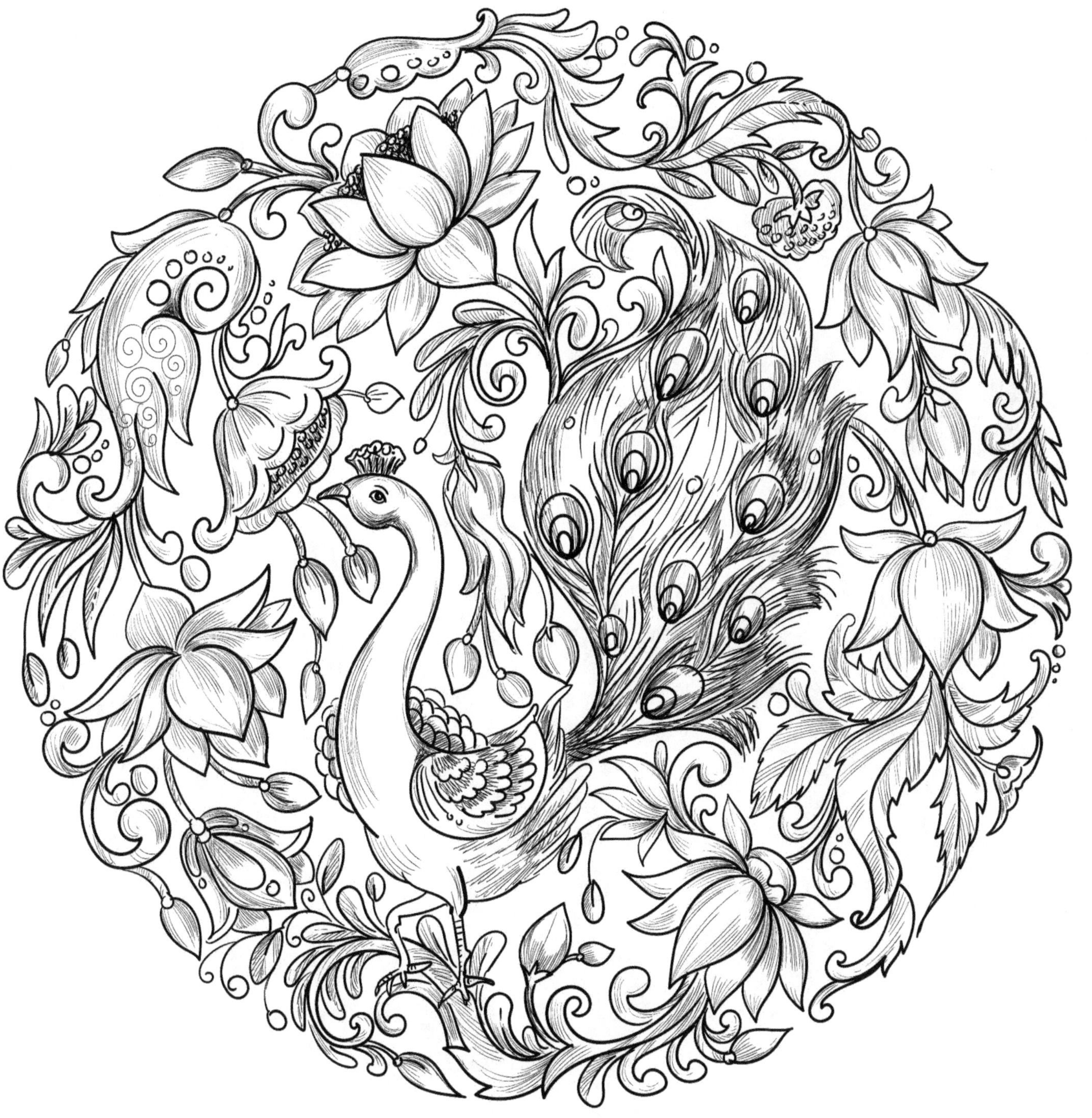

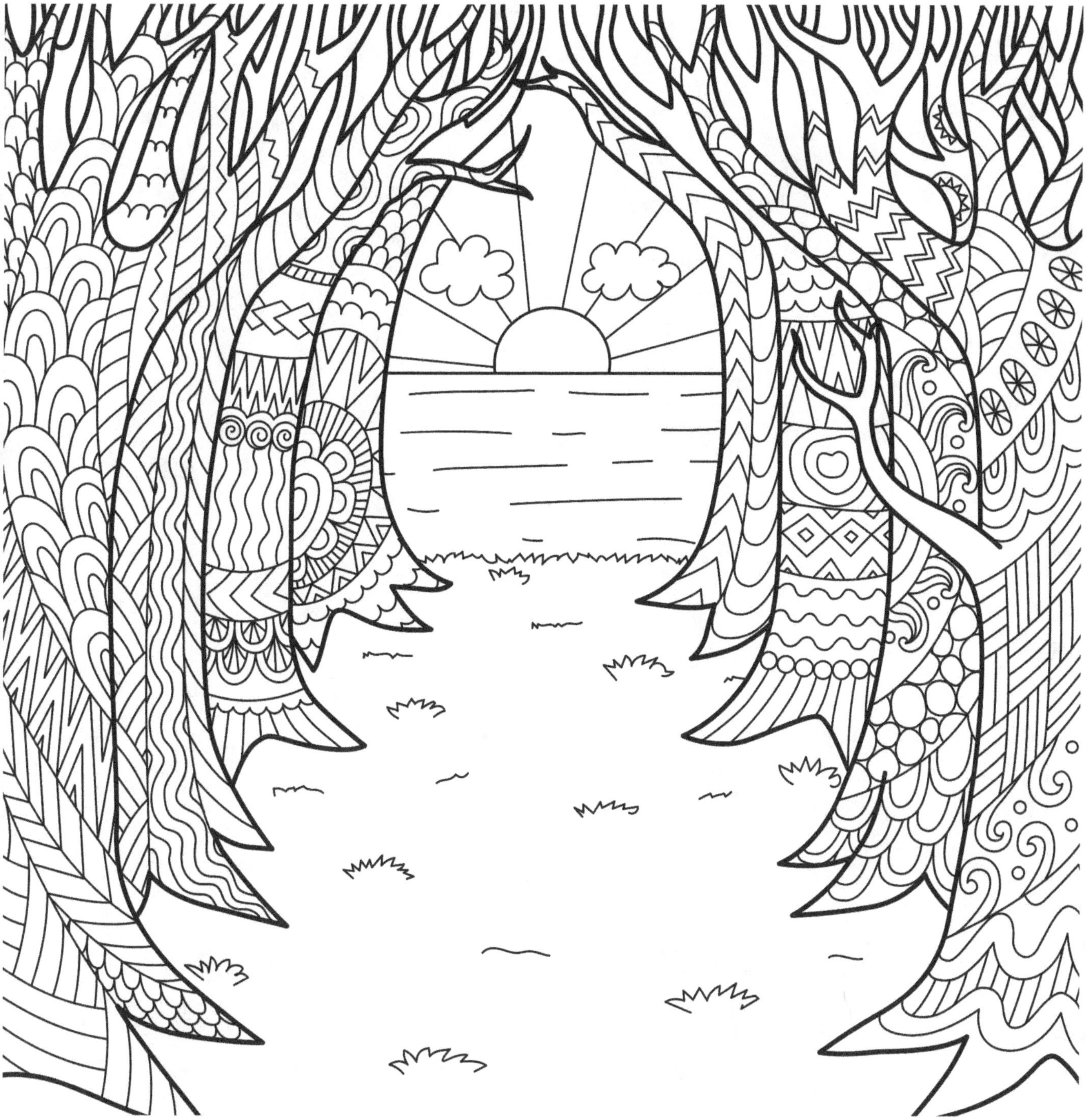

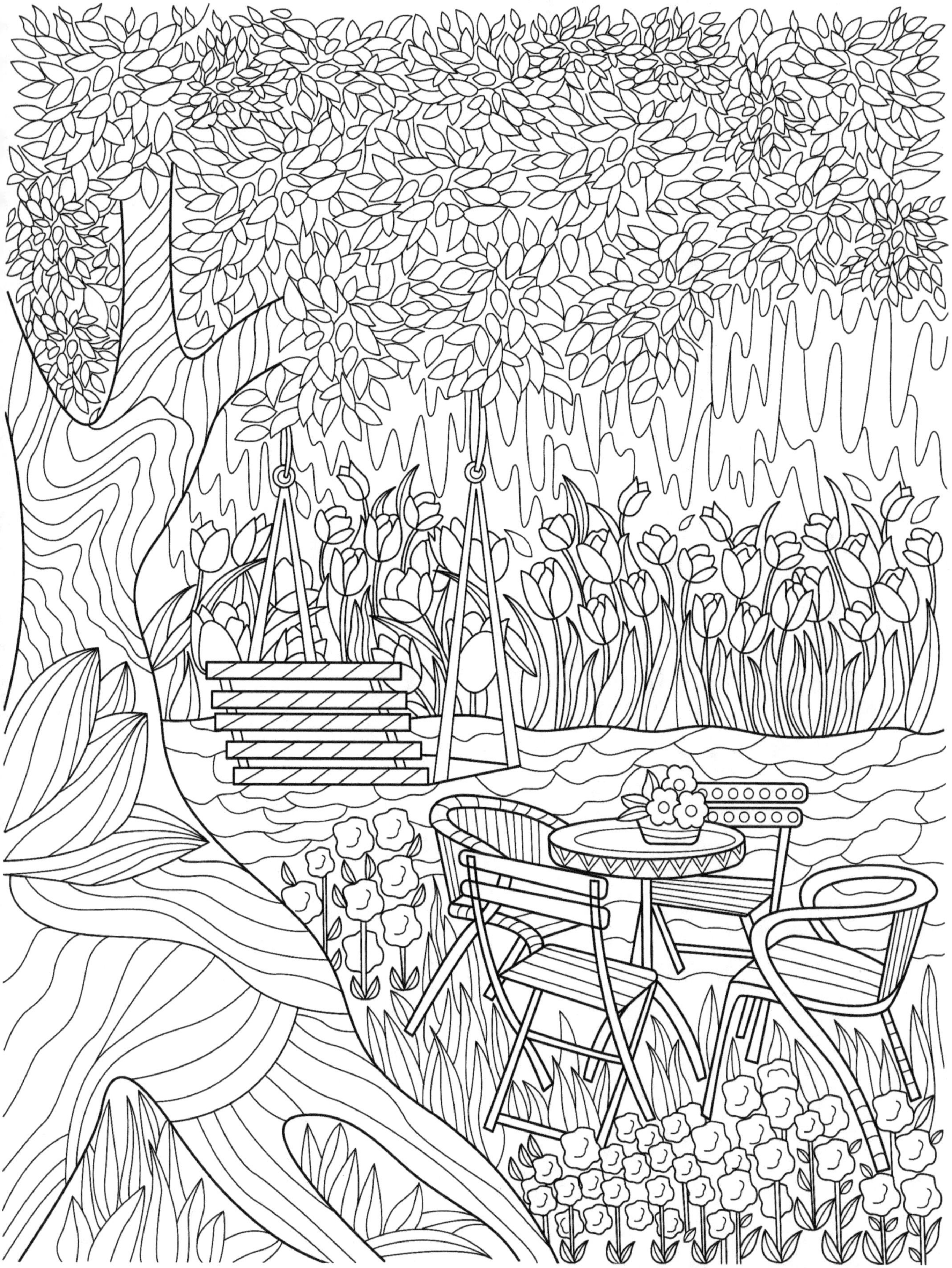

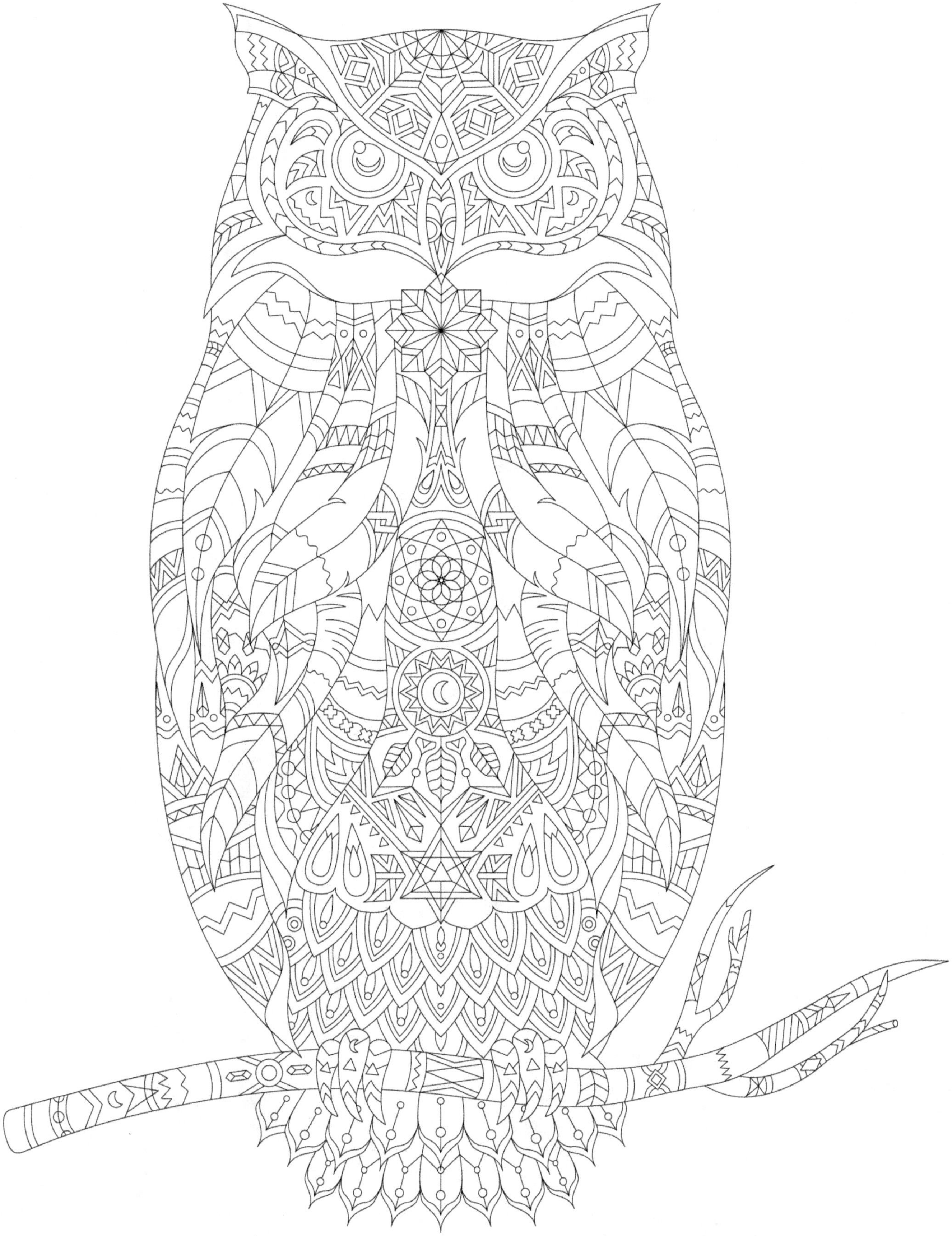

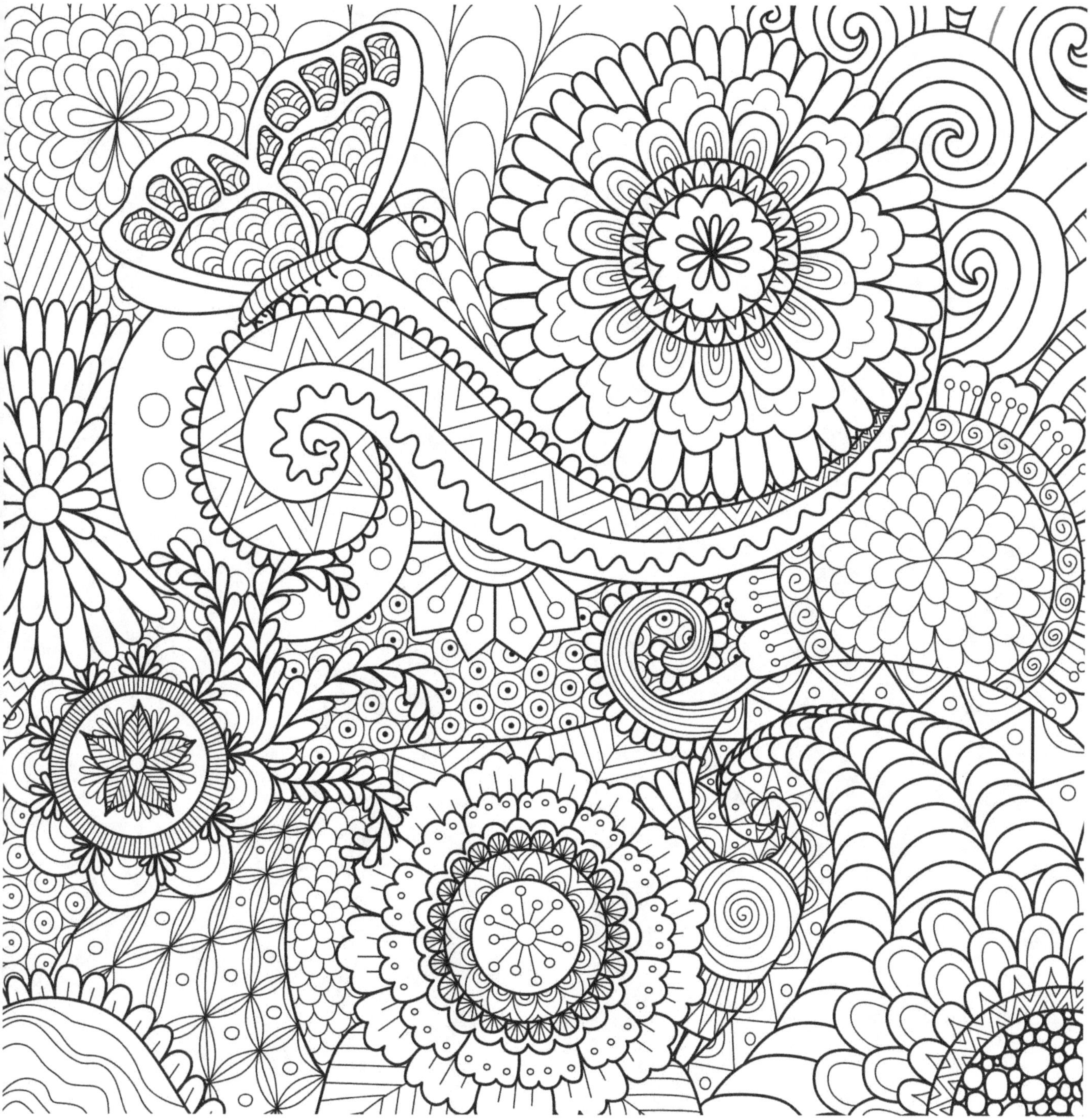

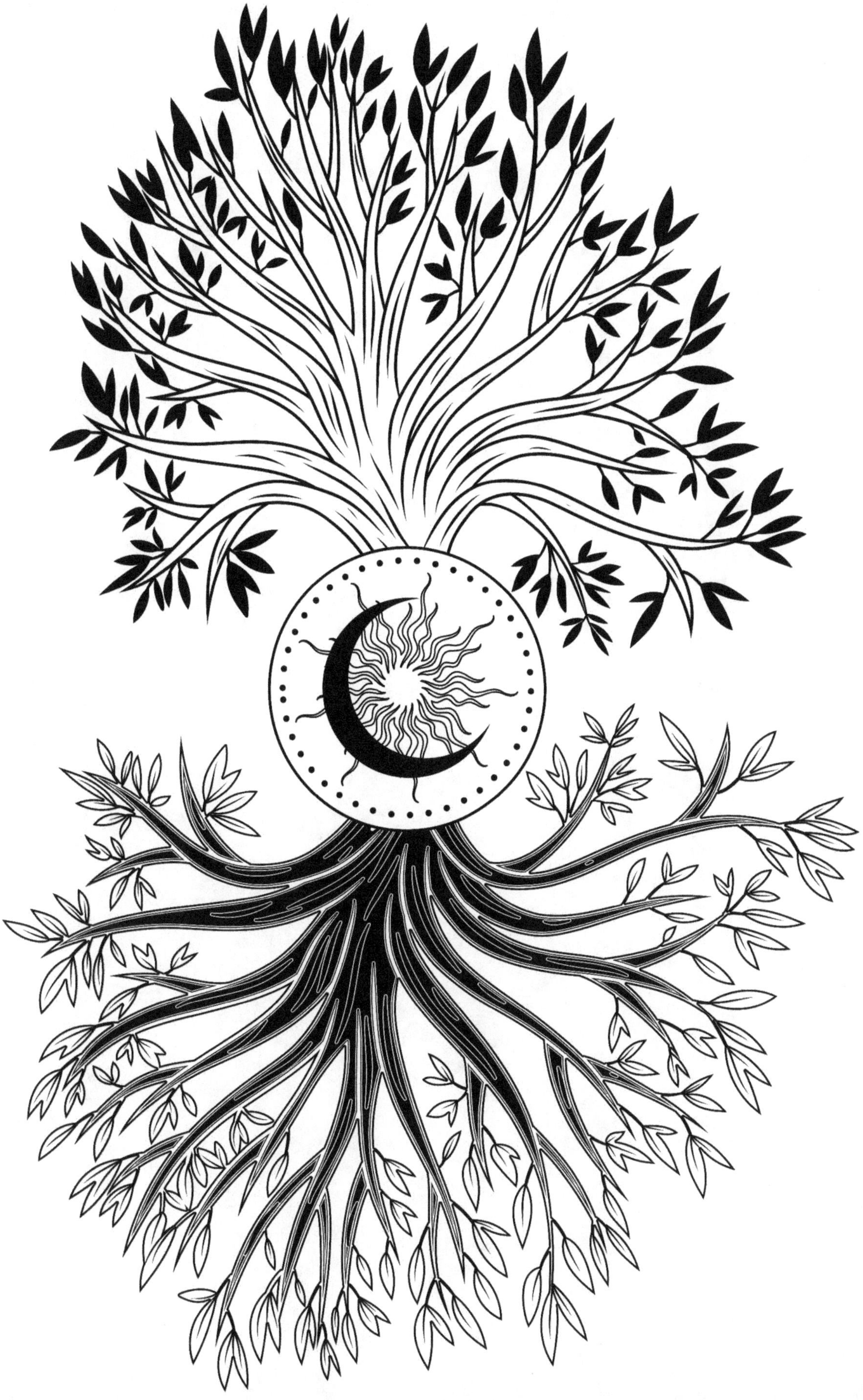

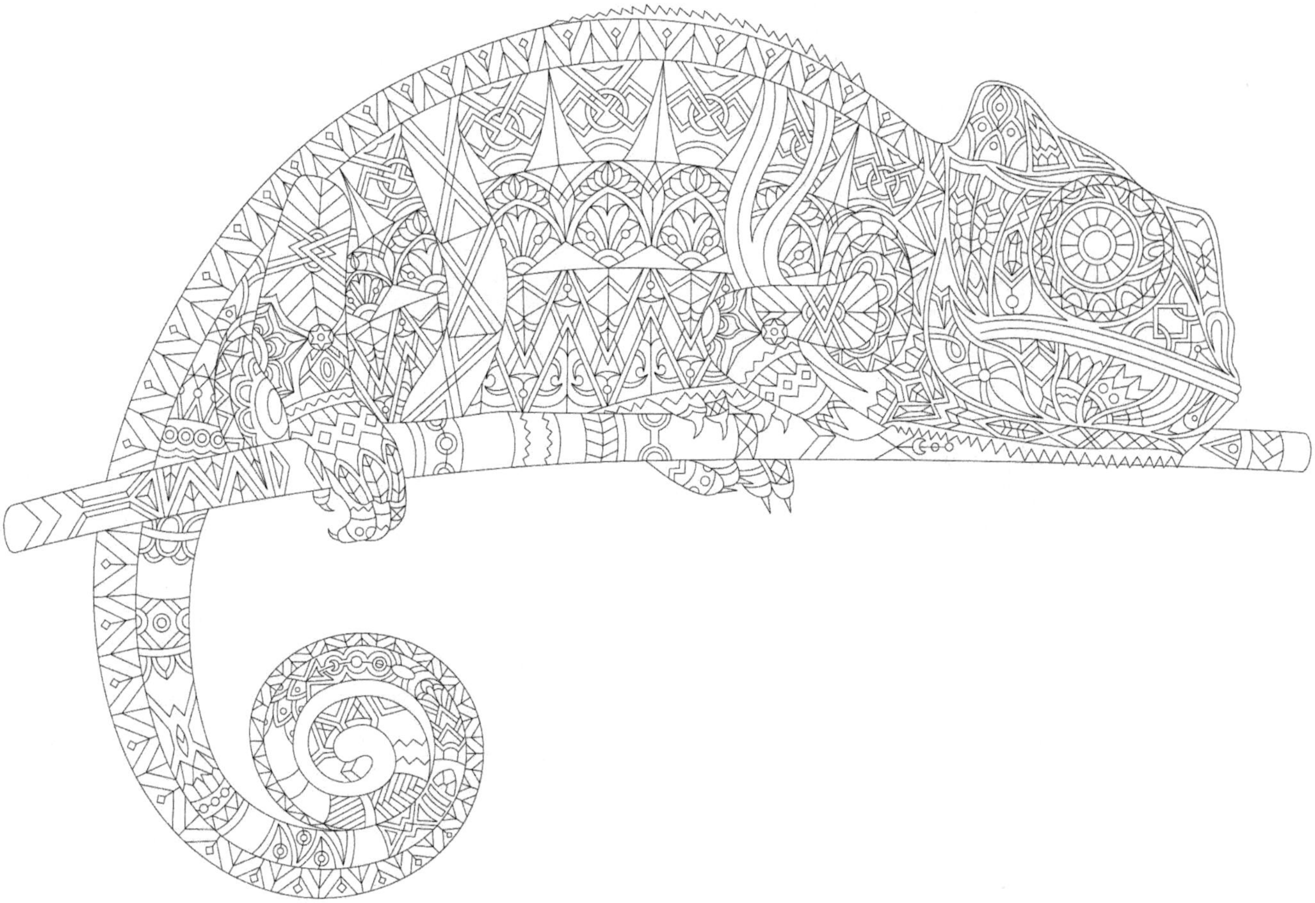

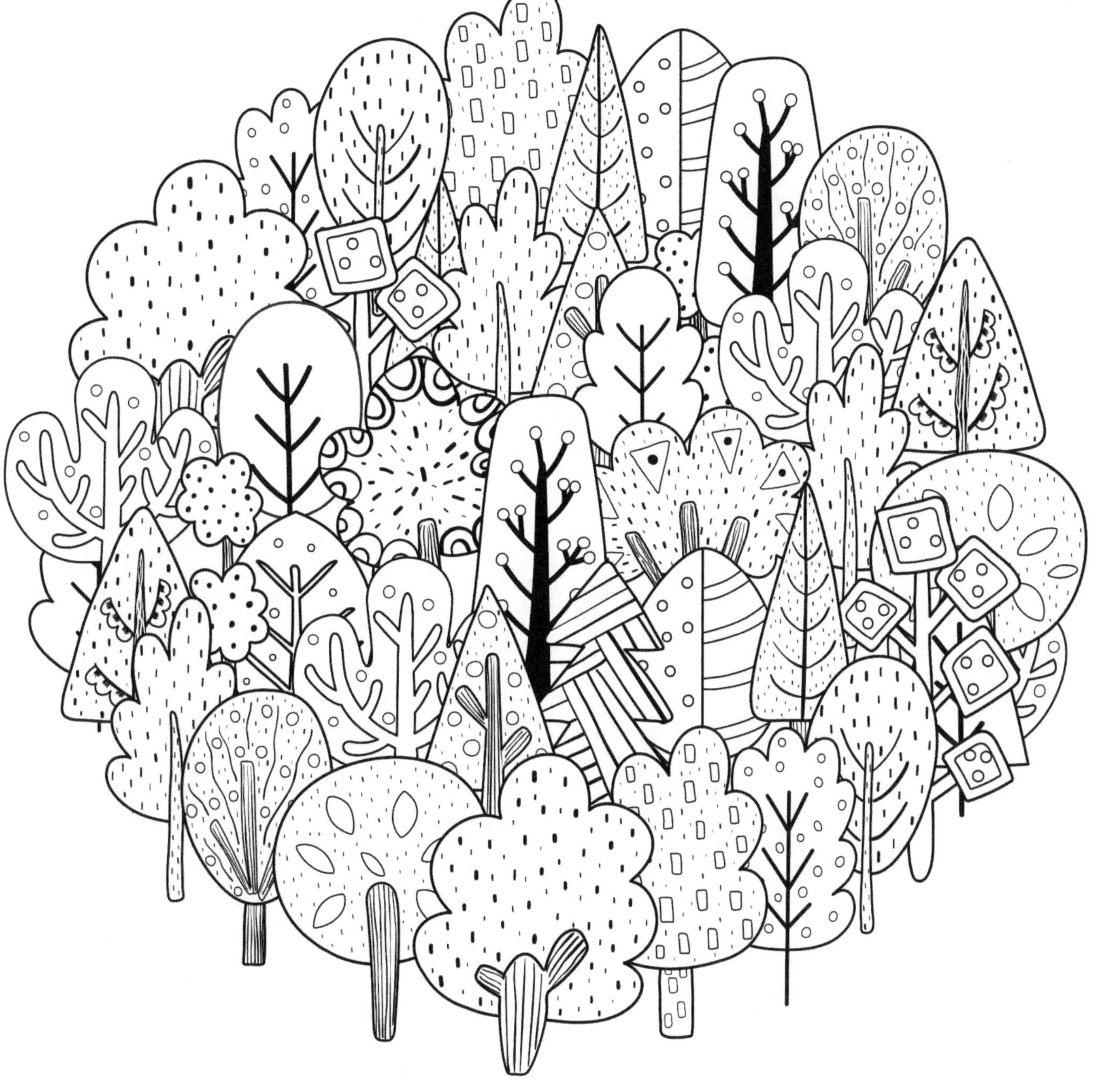

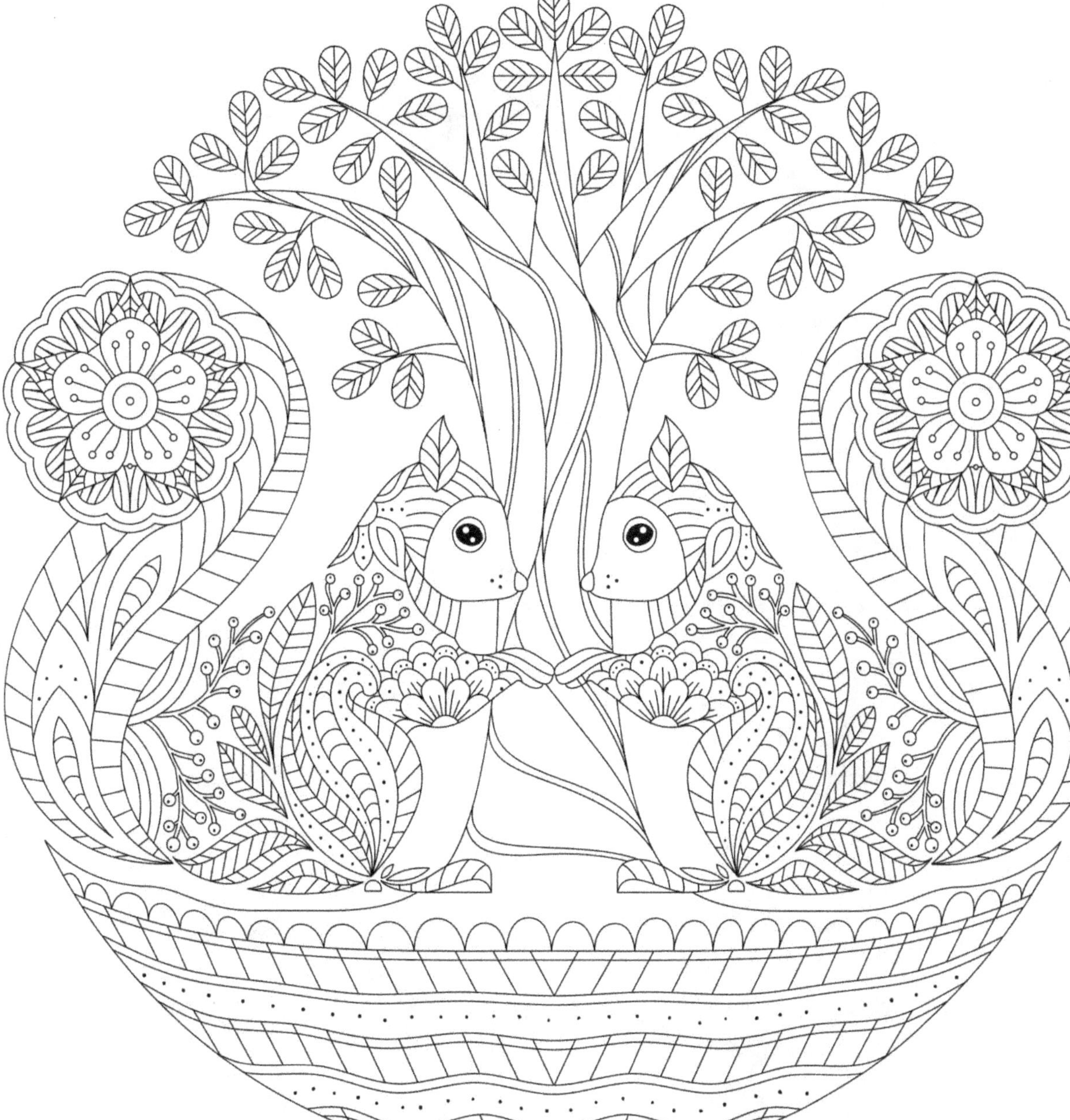

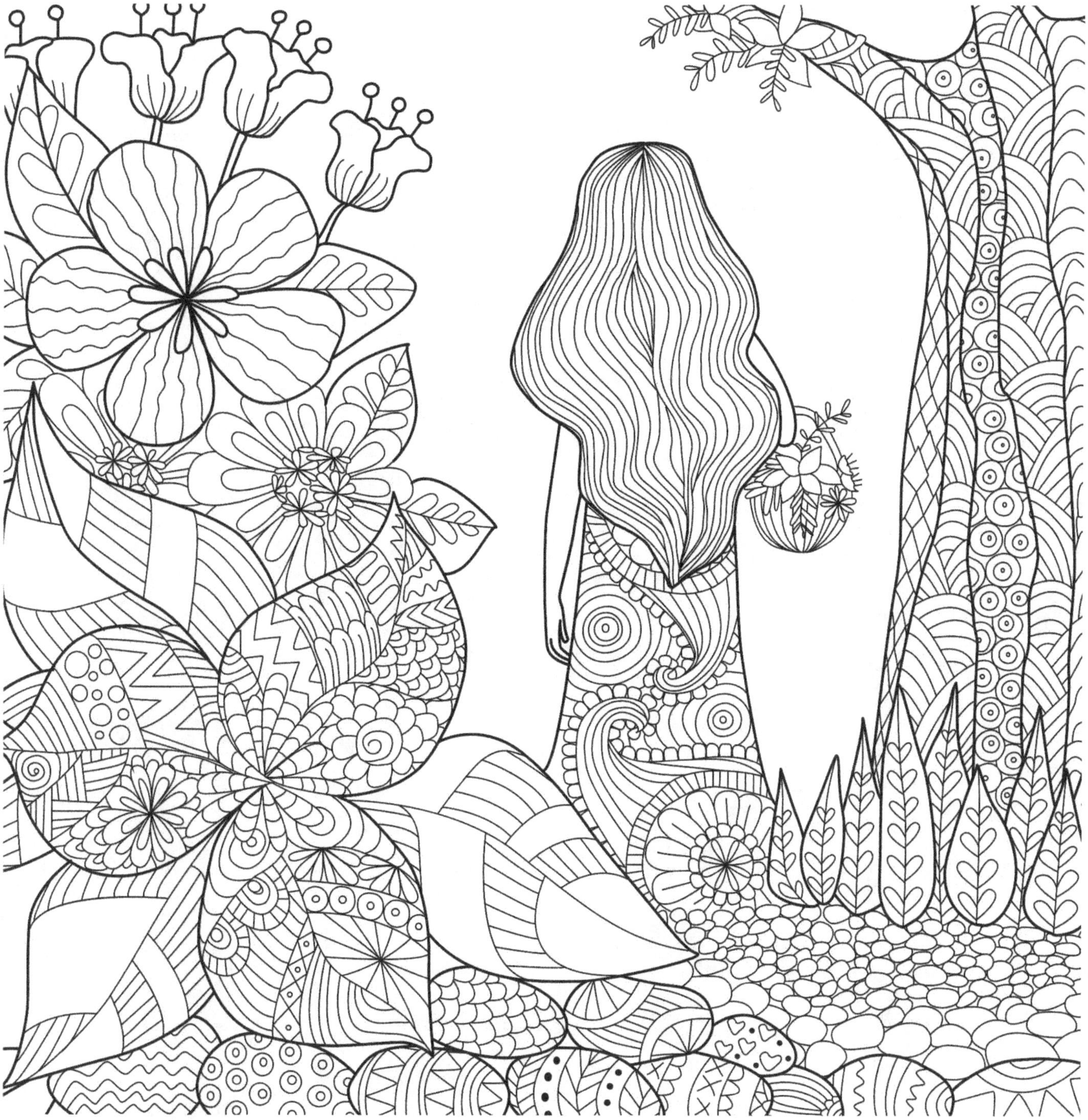

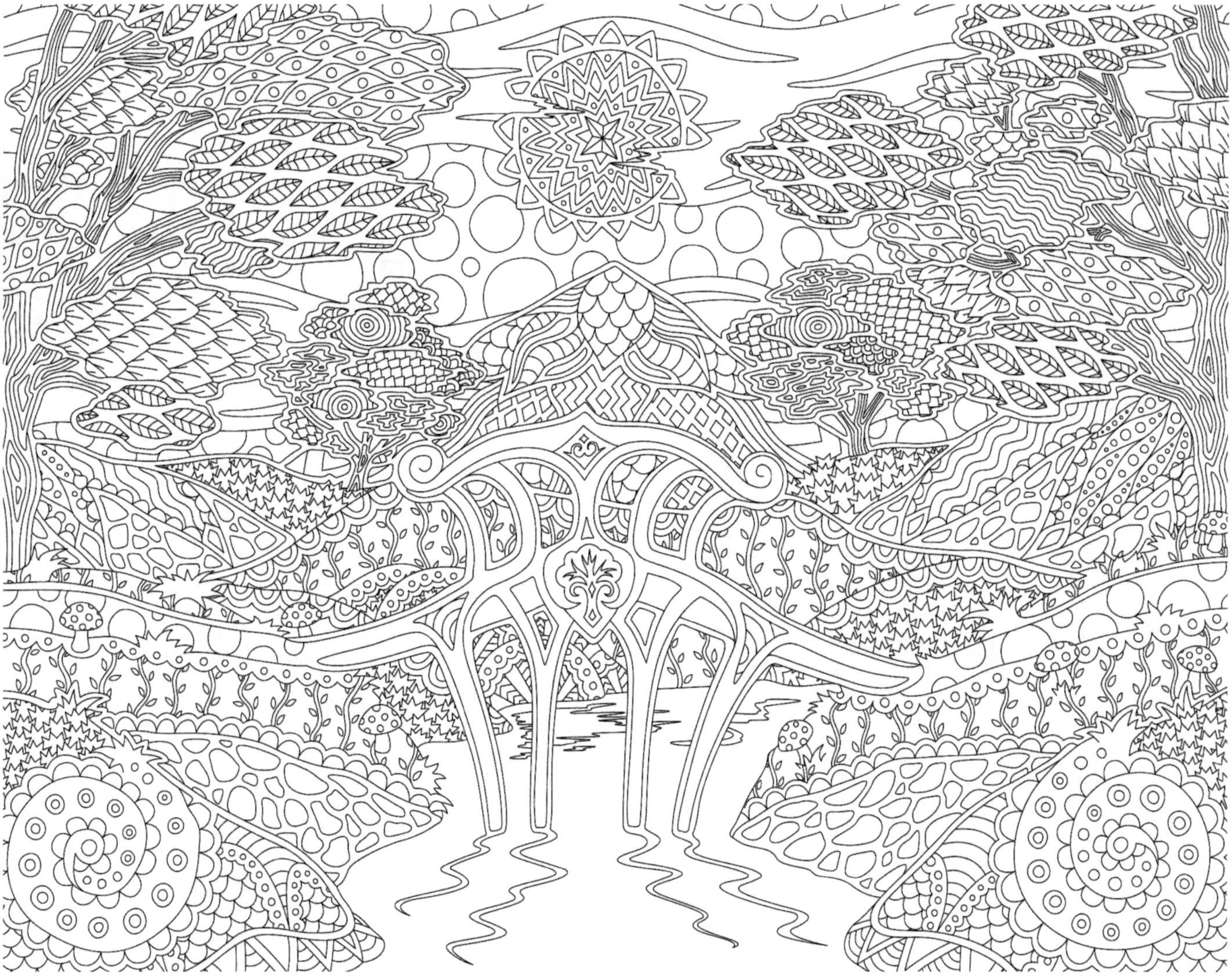

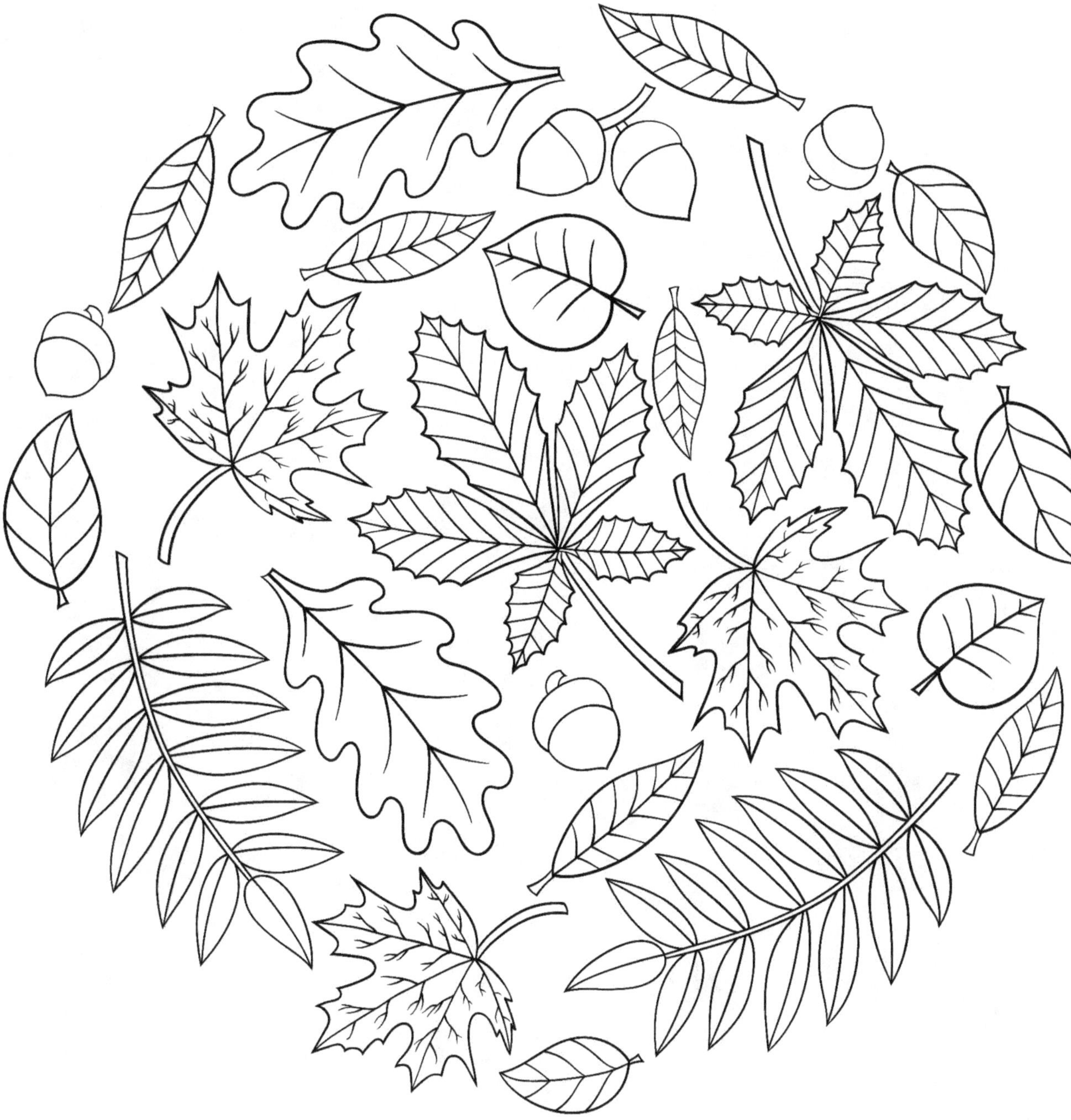

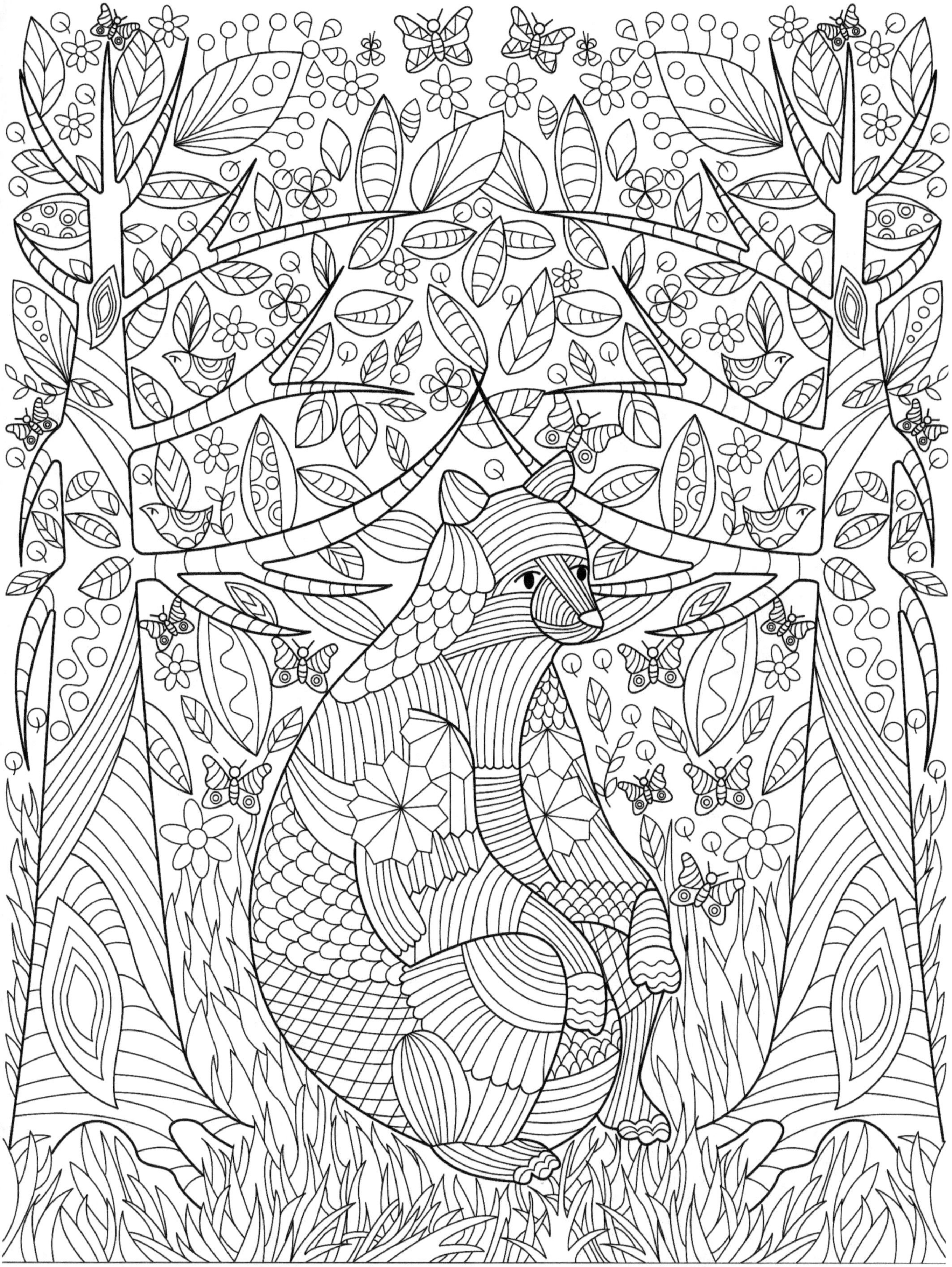

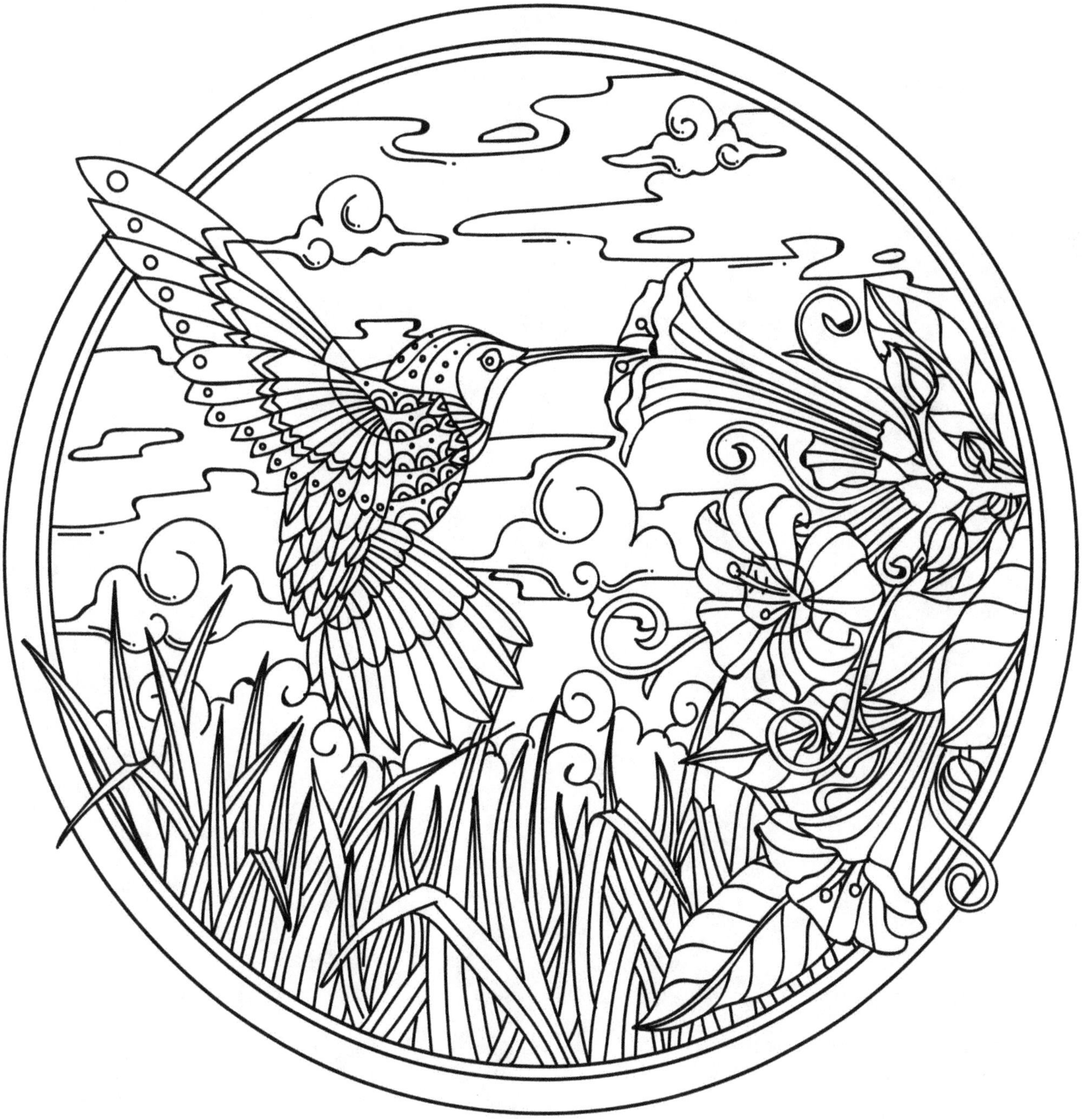

CPSIA information can be obtained
at www.ICGtesting.com
Printed in the USA
BVHW020615070723
666845BV00022B/497

9 798211 301641